BUILT FOR IMPACT

How Successful Nonprofits Lead, Execute, and Scale What Matters Most

Written by Doug Paul, Dr. Chris Curtis, Andy Graham, and Todd Milby

Cover design by Andy Graham and Givington's (Jeff Trojek)

Typeset and layout by Givington's (Jeff Trojek)

Graphic design by Andy Graham and Givington's (Jeff Trojek)

Printed in Canada through Givington's

First Edition, 2026

ISBN: 979-8-9935275-0-5

"This book is an amazing tool for any nonprofit leader and their executive team. It unpacks a powerful, practical, and simple system for running a successful nonprofit."

Abby Farris Rogers, Chief Development Officer, YMCA USA

"As a leader in a non-governmental organization with global impact, the proven concepts and strategies in *Built for Impact* resonate deeply. The ability to build and organize an ImpactOS—connecting passion with the right tools—is crucial for scaling a nonprofit's mission without losing its heart and soul."

Daniel Yang, Senior Director, World Relief

"These tools are transforming not just how our team operates, but how we think. Most importantly, they're helping us own and deliver measurable results for the schools and students we serve."

Ellen E. Weaver, State Superintendent of Education, State of South Carolina

"As a nonprofit executive who's explored several operating systems and leadership models over the years, I only wish I had discovered this one sooner. The tools are both practical and powerful. I'll be implementing them with my team starting tomorrow!"

Kristen Allender, Executive Director, Tennessee Kids Belong

"As an organization using the ImpactOS, our team feels the traction—and more importantly, we can now track it on a simple scoreboard, week after week."

Dave Ferguson, CEO, Exponential

"The care, creativity, and strategic intent behind this work are unmistakable. The thinking pushes into bold, genuinely innovative territory for the nonprofit sector while staying grounded in what nonprofits truly need to thrive. I'm deeply encouraged by the rigor, imagination, and purpose that shaped this effort."

Adrienne Wright Cleveland, Former Executive Director, U-Turn

"The book *Built for Impact* is written by people who truly understand the nonprofit world from the inside out. It captures what it feels like to lead an organization built around impact instead of profit—constant pressure, limited resources, and the fight to stay focused on what matters. The Impact Operating System gives language and structure to what most leaders have been improvising. It is practical without being corporate, and disciplined without being tone-deaf to mission. For anyone running a nonprofit that has outgrown instinct, this is the first framework that feels built for us."

Desiree Lee, President, FRAME Foundation

"This is an essential roadmap for every nonprofit."

David Bailey, Executive Director, Arrabon

"Having had the joy of working alongside this team as consultants—who I now consider friends—I can say the practical tools and process in *Built for Impac*t will help your organization not just survive, but thrive."

Dhati Lewis, President, MyBLVD

"This is the rare nonprofit guide written out of deep experience, not just theory—making it intensely practical and genuinely engaging. It's a powerful desktop reference tool, designed not as a one-time read but to provide the clear systems and actionable insights needed to consistently execute the mission you were called to complete."

Michael VanHuis, Executive Director, Missio Nexus

"Powerfully practical. Don't be surprised how quickly you'll start implementing rhythms, tools, and ideas in ways that help you get traction where it really matters. If clarity is kindness, then be kind to yourself and incorporate this book into your leadership so that your organization can actually get to where you have been longing to go."

Dave Ficken, LINC City Director Chicago

CONTENTS

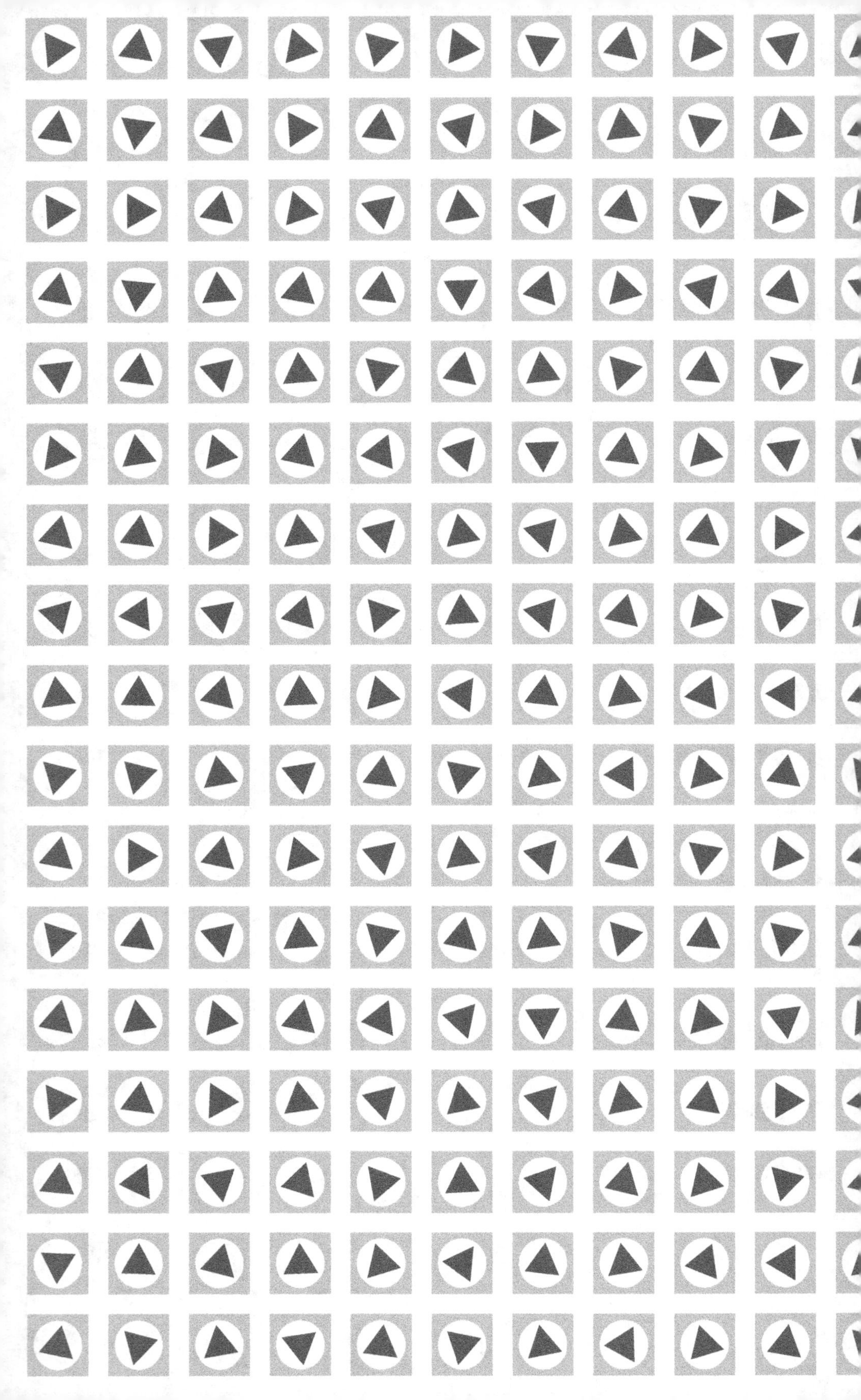

INTRODUCTION

Why You Got Into the Nonprofit Game

Leading a nonprofit is, hands down, one of the most challenging jobs out there.

You won't find it featured on Forbes' "Best Careers for the Future" list, though it should be. One reason is that it demands a rare blend of execution, compassion, sacrifice, inspiration, and resilience.

You are not just managing people, you are guiding them toward a mission that's bigger than any one person. You are not just solving problems, you are confronting injustices. All the while, you perform this invaluable work with fewer resources, greater scrutiny, and higher emotional stakes than practically every other sector.

Unlike the for-profit world, there are no quarterly reports that say, "We did it! We won!" Success is measured in changed lives, healthier communities, and restored dignity. These are transformation metrics that are far more difficult to track.

And yet, you chose this noble endeavor. Why? Because something within you simply would not, or could not, settle. Somewhere along the way, you witnessed something broken in the world and knew, deep down, something needed to change. You felt an unshakeable conviction that you were called to do something about it.

You chose sacrifice. You chose purpose. You decided to roll up your sleeves and commit to a kind of work that often defies explanation to those who haven't lived it. You saw the world as it is and believed in what could be. You were willing to step into the gap. That makes you rare.

But if this matters so much, why does it often feel so difficult?

Why Does It Often Feel So Difficult?

Not only have each of us led nonprofits, over the past two decades, we have also worked alongside more than 1,300 nonprofit organizations. We have felt the heavy load that leaders like you carry and have watched them do so with grace and grit. In all of those interactions, we have noticed at least five major points of difficulty for nonprofit leaders that appear again and again:

1. Leadership Sweet Spot

Nonprofit leaders are often pulled away from their core strengths. They may be dynamic visionaries, but suddenly they're also the *de facto* IT department or the newly minted accounting office. One leader told us, "I got into this to change lives, not to get buried in spreadsheets."

2. People

Leaders love the passion and sacrifice of their teams, yet discover that not everyone is a fit for the organization. Addressing this challenge can be heartbreaking, like telling a dedicated musician they're playing out of sync with the rest of the orchestra. Their passion is real, but the harmony is off, and it's affecting the whole performance. Some team members simply are not in the right seat, or they may not belong on the bus at all.

3. Finances

Fundraising in today's world feels like trying to nail Jell-O to a wall. Donor expectations are changing, digital tools are multiplying, and the line between nonprofit and business keeps blurring. You are trying to make the case for long-term impact in a short-term attention economy. Oh, and by the way, your livelihood—and that of your team—depends on it.

4. Change

Change used to happen gradually. Now it occurs between lunch and your 2:00 pm staff meeting. What worked five years ago feels ancient. It's exhausting knowing social media trends shift weekly, your CRM provider was bought out last week, the price is going up, and your interns know more about AI than your consultants. Strategies that worked a decade ago might now be as relevant as dial-up internet. The team clings to old models that yield diminishing returns. Meanwhile, the rest of the world leaps forward, embracing new engagement tools, leaving you with the thought, "Wait, we're still using that?"

5. Growth

For nonprofits aiming to expand, the complexities balloon. You are not just producing more widgets; you are trying to replicate nuanced relational work in new communities. Doing so often requires a map that hasn't yet been written, leaving you to make it up as you go, hoping not to lose the essence that made you effective in the first place.

Precisely for these reasons, and more, we created the Impact Operating System.

The Impact OS is a customizable set of tools, principles, and frameworks designed to help you lead your organization with clarity and effectiveness.

This is not just another business framework. It's a way of working, leading, and growing that is built for nonprofits like yours: mission-driven, people-centric, and impact-obsessed.

It's a nonprofit-specific playbook that helps you sprint towards the vision you carry, with a system that has heart, remains human, and amplifies passion rather than killing it.

Meet Trayvon.*

Trayvon was the kind of student every teacher hopes for: bright, focused, and naturally gifted. He breezed through high school, majored in business, and after paying his dues in the early years of his career, he landed a great job and quickly climbed the corporate ladder. By forty-one, he had it all: the family, the title, the salary, the corner office.

And yet...he felt empty. Restless. He was looking to give himself to something that really mattered.

On weekends, he began volunteering at a nonprofit that helps people recently released from prison find housing, employment, and the community support they need to rebuild their lives. The work wasn't glamorous, but it was deeply human. This organization didn't just wish folks luck; they walked with them into the next chapter, offering dignity and direction.

For Trayvon, it struck a nerve. When he was growing up, his uncle made a significant mistake at nineteen that nearly derailed his life. Trayvon always loved him, and now he saw his uncle's story mirrored in those he served. It wasn't abstract anymore...it was personal.

Soon, weekends bled into weeknights. He ran financial models for the development team, mentored participants, and even sat in on strategic meetings just to help. So when the longtime Executive Director announced her retirement, the choice was obvious. Trayvon had the heart, the head, and the team's trust.

He said yes, and the early days were electric. Ideas flowed. Morale soared. Fundraising efforts gained traction.

But by year five, reality hit. They weren't failing, but they weren't moving forward either. Despite working harder than ever, it felt like running in place.

Something just wasn't working.

---

*This book draws on real-world experiences from years of working alongside nonprofit leaders, teams, and organizations. To honor the privacy and confidentiality of those involved, the names, roles, and identifying details have been changed throughout.

Just when Trayvon was ready to give up (or at least search "sabbatical programs for burnt-out nonprofit leaders"), a friend in the for-profit world shared how their company had turned a corner with an organizational operating system. Trayvon was intrigued. He tried adapting some of those tools. A few helped, but most didn't fit. It was like wearing his dad's suit to prom – noble effort, but wrong fit.

That's when we met Trayvon. We introduced him to the principles found in the Impact Operating System: a framework and playbook built for nonprofits, not borrowed from business. A system designed to hold both the passion and the practical—the heart and the how. He dove in.

Just a year later, the change was undeniable. Board meetings were sharper. Staff meetings had rhythm. Goals weren't just set; they were tracked, measured, and celebrated. Fundraising and volunteer retention were up, but do you know what happened that was the most important?

The mission. The mission was moving forward, bringing their vision closer to reality.

Recidivism rates dropped. Local businesses asked to partner. One graduate said, "You didn't just help me get a job. You helped me become a man again."

Trayvon found renewed hope and rediscovered the joy of leading with purpose.

Maybe you're here because you feel what he once felt – close, but perhaps a little stuck. You've tried plans and borrowed business systems, but they didn't quite fit.

For over 20 years, we've seen the principles of the Impact Operating System give leaders like Trayvon and nonprofits like yours the clarity, alignment, and impact they long for.

It can do the same for you.

Before You Start This Book

At the ImpactCo, we believe that if every nonprofit achieves the vision and mission for which they feel responsible, the world would become a much, much better place. Like you, we believe the world needs good people racing towards big problems with heart and hustle to do something about it. There is something in these leaders that says, "the world is broken and it shouldn't be this way." We want to give these leaders what they need to succeed because it's actually not that mysterious! So everything in this book came out of a heart to give leaders like you the practical tools you need to carry out what you feel responsible for.

The Impact Operating System draws inspiration from a host of thinkers, practitioners, and innovators across the social sector (and beyond). We have spent more than two decades refining, honing, and customizing the principles, tools, and tactics. We have also had the privilege of implementing it with leaders like you.

Rather than creating a system you have to adopt wholesale, we've created something customizable to your DNA, mission, and convictions. It is a flexible toolkit you can tailor to your organization's unique DNA, whether you are serving local families in crisis or advocating for international policy changes.

A few things to keep in mind as you read:

1. We encourage you to keep a notebook or digital doc handy while you read for the purpose of making notes on how each concept can adapt to your mission.

2. As a companion to this book, we have created a Starter Kit that includes digital templates, worksheets, detailed instructions, and coaching videos to help you along the way. It will bring clarity to the tools that we will introduce to you and spark imagination about how you could integrate them into your organization. These additions are free and accessible through the QR code below.

3. We have created a native app called ImpactHub that works on your phone, iPad, or desktop. The entire app is built specifically for the ImpactOS.

   To get more info, check out: ImpactNonprofit.com/app

If your goal is to expand your nonprofit's influence and deepen your impact without sacrificing the joy of leading, this book is for you. We cannot promise it will be easy, as nonprofit leadership never is, but we can promise it will be far more fruitful and (dare we say) even a bit more fun. When your staff, board, and volunteers align around a customized operating system, you free yourself to focus on why you got into the game in the first place: changing lives and transforming communities.

Now, let's begin the journey together.

Let's unlock the potential of your nonprofit, one system, one strategy, one tool at a time. Your mission demands it. Your team needs it, and the communities you serve are counting on it.

1

THE IMPACT OPERATING SYSTEM

You do not rise to the ambition of your vision; you fall to the level of your systems.

Did you know that 71% of nonprofits are failing to achieve their stated mission?

You won't find this statistic memorialized on a bronze plaque. And if we are honest, all of us have had moments in leading a nonprofit when we found ourselves wondering whether our organization might be edging uncomfortably close to increasing that statistic.

Whether your nonprofit feels stuck, strained, or surging with momentum, one thing is true: everyone is looking for a way to increase impact and effectiveness. In that search, nonprofit leaders often find themselves chasing the next big fix. Maybe it's a new strategic plan, a star advancement officer, or a promising new program. But too often, they're looking for a silver bullet - one magic solution to solve every challenge.

One reason leaders often look for the mythical silver bullet is that they are passionate about their Vision to change their community by helping people who need it most. But that passion can only take you so far. Eventually, you need some way to bring your Vision to life.

Here is the reality: You do not rise to the ambition of your vision; you fall to the level of your systems.

After reading that last sentence containing the word "system", many of you will hear "bureaucracy," "red tape," or "soul sucking rules and processes." Maybe worst of all, you hear "corporate efficiency." We understand those sentiments and often agree with them when we see how some nonprofits attempt to implement business systems within their organizations.

Nonprofit leaders like you want to hold in tension both structure and freedom—outcomes and heart. You want to live in the beautiful, messy middle of the continuum. On one end of the continuum is *Structure,*

Systems & Impact Outcomes, and on the other end are *Passion*, *Freedom*, and *Flexibility*.

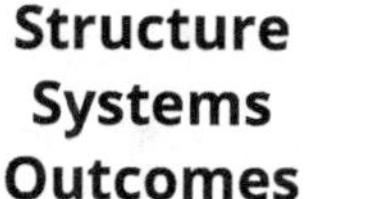

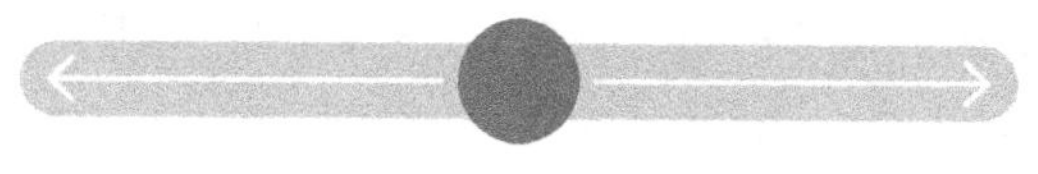

Passion
Freedom
Flexibility

We are convinced you need something that helps you achieve the mission while still leaving room for freedom and passion. You need just enough structure to thrive, not suffocate. You need repeatable rhythms that support the real work rather than adding to it.

You need just enough structure to thrive, not suffocate.

You need an Organizational Operating System.

What Is an Organizational Operating System

An organizational operating system is a set of frameworks, processes, and tools that help everyone in an organization move in the same direction. Think of it as your internal GPS. It doesn't tell everyone where to go; it just helps everyone agree on how to get there.

Now, when we say operating system, we don't mean technology. It's more like the playbook your whole organization runs on – the rhythms, habits, and tools you use every day. Every nonprofit already has one (whether you realize it or not), so the real question is this: "Is it helping or holding you back?"

Here's the million-dollar question: What playbook are most nonprofits running on?

For decades, many nonprofit organizations have tried to solve nonprofit problems with business-world solutions. Well-meaning board members and proactive C-suite leaders have attempted to adopt and adapt those solutions. But business playbooks are built to generate profit; nonprofits need a playbook built for impact.

One of the most well-known operating systems in the business world is the Entrepreneurial Operating System (EOS), made popular by the book Traction. Over 300,000 businesses use it today, and for good reason. EOS is an excellent framework for companies pursuing profit and growth.

For years, we used EOS with nonprofits, adapting and tweaking where we could. But over time, we kept running into friction points that wouldn't go away. It was like sand in the gears. No matter how hard the leaders worked, the system kept grinding.

The challenges leaders face with business-world solutions showed up in ways that every nonprofit leader will recognize:

- Boards second-guessing decisions but dodging engagement or accountability
- Volunteers ghosting commitments, but they're a work force you have to rely on
- Fundraising tied to donor agendas, not organizational priorities
- Passionate teams stretched thin and burning out fast
- Talented leaders stuck in endless planning with little execution

These aren't minor frustrations. They are structural challenges that run deeply through the unique DNA of nonprofit life. The more we tried to retrofit a business tool for nonprofit realities, the clearer it became: we needed a system built from the ground up for nonprofit impact.

Then we asked ourselves, "What do the most successful, sustainable, and mission-advancing nonprofits have in common?"

We replayed rooms we have been in over the last 20 years, from small conference spaces to big boardrooms, volunteer kitchens, and national hubs. We looked past the slogans, different-sized budgets, and varying missions. And then it clicked: there weren't fifty things they had in common. There weren't even twelve. There were eight. Only eight! The same eight kept showing up repeatedly in organizations that endured pressure, grew with integrity, and delivered outcomes people could see. Once we saw it, we captured the pattern and built a simple system around it.

Not retrofitted.

Not repurposed.

Something that speaks the language of mission-driven, human-centered nonprofit work.

That system is the Impact Operating System.

A successful nonprofit has a transformative mission, healthy culture, and sustainable operations.

The Impact Operating System

The Impact Operating System is the only customizable framework specifically designed for nonprofit leadership, management, and execution. Think of it as the best of proven organizational design principles, plus the flexibility and passion essential for leading a nonprofit with your specific DNA.

To illustrate how this works, think of a rotary engine. These engines run with elegant simplicity, yet they contain parts calibrated to work harmoniously together. When that happens, it produces smooth, sustained power output with only three basic moving parts: frame, rotors, and drive shaft.

A Rotary Engine

Similarly, the Impact Operating System drives nonprofits forward through eight streamlined components: Vision, Development, Strategy, Metrics, Culture, People, Systems, and Rhythms. Each of the eight core components fits together to drive you toward greater impact.

While a nonprofit may juggle dozens of complex roles, challenges, and programs, the system is designed to function seamlessly through its simplicity. If one component is misaligned, the entire machine can sputter. (In fact, this one little insight might name years of frustration you've experienced.)

What we have learned is that most teams have a few of the eight components in place (often done instinctively), a few that are present but underbuilt, and two or three that are missing altogether. When components are missing or underbuilt, it can feel like this:

- **Vision:** Your Vision sounds good, but you're getting lukewarm results.
- **Strategy:** Your team is bustling, but you're not getting momentum.
- **Development:** Every year, it's harder to raise the same amount of money.
- **Metrics:** You're not sure you're measuring the right things in the right way.
- **Culture:** Unintentional culture undermines great teams.
- **People:** Role confusion and bottlenecks across staff, board, and volunteers.
- **Systems:** Dropped balls, last-minute scrambles, and something is always on fire.
- **Rhythms:** Wildly inconsistent execution, quality, and accountability.

The Impact Operating System Components

Vision

Strategy

Culture

People

Systems

Rhythms

Metrics

Development

ImpactOS Component Cheat Sheet

Component	What's Required	Master Tool	Problem this is Trying to Solve
Vision	A clear, 5-year, attainable slice of the big vision	Moonshot Tool	Your vision sounds good but you're getting luke-warm results.
Strategy	A flexible action plan linked to a winning strategy.	Impact Roadmap	Your team is really busy but you're not getting momentum.
Development	A modern revenue playbook built for your DNA.	FUEL Matrix	Every year it's harder to raise the same amount of money.
Metrics	A scorecard with lead and lag impact measures.	Impact Dashboard	You're not sure you're measuring the right things in the right way.
Culture	Shared agreement on "how we work together."	Culture Making Tool	Unintentional culture undermines great teams.
People	The right people in the right seats of the bus.	Right Fit Tool Org Chart Analyzer DARCI Board Tune Up Tool	Role confusion and bottlenecks across staff, board, and volunteers.
Systems	Simple, repeatable core processes documented and followed.	7 VIP Tool	Dropped balls, last-minute scrambles, and something is always on fire.
Rhythms	Repeatable cadences that trigger impact outcomes.	Impact Calendar	Inconsistent execution, quality, and accountability.

In the chapters that follow, you will discover how to create light structures while maintaining flexibility by integrating each component to create your organization's customized OS. This gives you the ability to maximize your team's passion while ensuring the mission scales effectively.

But first, here's a high-level overview of each of the eight components.

Vision

You've heard Vision discussed a thousand times, but here's the problem: the Visions of most nonprofits sound inspiring, but often do nothing to drive real progress. They're too vague, too lofty, or too generic to guide action. Put another way, *the Vision lacks teeth*.

To address this challenge, we will introduce you to the Moonshot Tool, a framework that helps you craft a Vision that is meaningful, memorable, and measurable. *It's about having Vision with teeth*. You'll combine your passion, your unique superpower, and your community's urgent needs into a clear, bold, time-bound target. This becomes the "North Star" your team can rally behind. No more guessing where you are going. This tool shows you how to articulate a Vision that makes people want to join, give, and stay.

Strategy

Strategy is often misunderstood in the nonprofit space. It's not about long documents or fancy buzzwords. It's about answering the question: *How will we get from where we are now to the future we envision?*

We will introduce the concept of a *winning strategy* through the Impact Roadmap, which will help you create a clear, actionable plan. The Impact Roadmap breaks your Moonshot into 3-year outcomes, 1-year "must wins," and 90-day priorities. These are not goals that live in a file: they live in your meetings, your daily decision-making, and hallway conversations.

Strategy becomes something your whole team understands, owns, and moves forward together. They become even stronger because they can flex and grow. As you test it and learn more, the change doesn't shatter the plan; it strengthens it.

Development

If you've ever asked, "How can we fund this mission?" you're not alone. Development isn't about chasing shiny objects or pulling off a big gala. It's about aligning your people, messaging, donor engagement, and a development playbook to sustain the mission long term.

The FUEL Matrix helps you diagnose where your development efforts stand across nine verticals (such as major gifts or recurring donors) and determine your current level (101-401). Then, you build a fundraising strategy aligned with your capacity and community, not a copy-and-paste from someone else's playbook. This tool will help you identify and fix the gaps that keep your development efforts stuck in survival mode.

Metrics

You want to know if your work is making a difference, but the numbers can feel overwhelming, irrelevant, or confusing. Worse, many teams track the wrong data in the wrong way, leading to "spreadsheet fatigue" and unclear direction.

This chapter introduces the Impact Dashboard and Metrics Tracker. These tools help you focus on the 9–15 key measurables that matter most. You'll learn to distinguish between *lead measures* (what you control) and *lag measures* (the results), giving you early warning signals and clearer insights, with step-by-step instructions for building your Impact Dashboard. The right metrics bring clarity, not confusion, and give your team confidence that they are on track to real-world impact.

Culture

Culture often gets dismissed as a "soft" issue. But in a sector fueled by passion, it is frequently the *only* thing that keeps a team going when resources are scarce and stress is high. Culture is not something you *have*—it's something you *build*. Therefore, culture making is not a nicety; it's a necessity for nonprofit leaders.

This chapter introduces the Culture-Making Tool, which helps you intentionally craft the way your team shows up and works together. You'll define the cultural building blocks that align with your mission and values. Whether onboarding new staff or reinvigorating your existing team, this tool helps create a culture where people thrive, not just survive.

People

People are your greatest asset and sometimes your most significant pain point. Managing staff, boards, donors, and volunteers often feels like herding cats across a minefield. Misalignment leads to confusion, resentment, and wasted effort.

In this chapter, you'll meet four transformative tools:

1. The Right Fit Tool: who belongs and who doesn't
2. Board Tune-Up: aligns your board with your mission, strategy, and team
3. DARCI Framework: clarifies everyone's role in decision-making and execution
4. Org Chart Analyzer: keeps your structure relevant and opportunistic

Together, these tools clarify roles, decisions, and expectations, freeing your team to focus on delivering impact rather than managing dysfunction.

Systems

You don't want to grow chaos, much less scale it. If your team is constantly reinventing how to send a newsletter or onboard a volunteer, you're bleeding time, trust, and talent. Strong systems protect and amplify passion rather than smother it.

We will show you how to identify your 7VIPs (Seven Very Important Processes) and build simple, documented workflows around them, helping you choose the right places to focus your consistency. Whether it's event planning, thank-you notes, or new hire onboarding, these repeatable processes become your "recipes for success." Systems reduce the noise, increase consistency, and help your mission scale without burning everyone out. And this, in turn, produces freedom to focus on the mission that nonprofit staff crave.

Rhythms

Nonprofit teams often have a lot of passion but struggle to maintain focus and momentum. Without precise execution rhythms, even the best-laid plans fizzle out.

The ImpactOS solution? A handful of simple, structured, repeatable rhythms. The Weekly Impact Check-In is a 90-minute team rhythm that reinforces short-term priorities, celebrates wins, and identifies what's stuck. Combine that with monthly one-on-ones and quarterly resets that intersect with your customized Impact OS, and you've got a cadence that keeps people aligned and energized. This is about creating flow rather than a bureaucracy. Execution rhythms ensure your strategy gains traction and your Vision becomes reality.

In many ways, Rhythms serve as the core element that unifies the entire system. Chapter 11 will show how all the components integrate into a powerful, well-oiled engine.

Before You Turn the Page

The mission is never easy, but it shouldn't be this hard.

We've worked with enough leaders to know that sooner or later, you'll hit a wall in leading your nonprofit. Maybe you're reading this because you just hit it! That's normal and to be expected. But here's what we want you to know:

The mission is never going to be easy, but it shouldn't be this hard.

When the work feels heavy, it is usually the weight of old habits, unclear roles, and accidental systems, not a lack of heart.

We created the Impact Operating System to help leaders like you navigate inflection points and pivotal moments with confidence. It is designed to help you accomplish the Vision for which you feel responsible. Whether you're leading a national nonprofit with a thousand staff or a small community-based group of volunteers, the principles remain the same: clarity, alignment, and, eventually...*momentum*.

If you happen to be a small nonprofit leader, a quick word of encouragement as you read on. You may feel overwhelmed as you wonder how you could possibly integrate this system wholesale. We understand that sentiment. However, in the pages that follow, you will find practical steps to increase your impact, no matter your size. Not only that, but at the end of this book, we have outlined some simple ways we can partner with you. So, keep reading. It will be worth it.

What's Your Current Baseline? Take Our Free Assessment

At this point, it would be helpful to take our free digital assessment. It provides a comprehensive baseline of your organization's standing across the eight core components. Our proprietary reporting platform, built on the Impact Operating System, will give you clarity on immediate priorities and highlight your organization's unique strengths. Knowing your current reality is the first step to mapping a strategy that truly amplifies your impact.

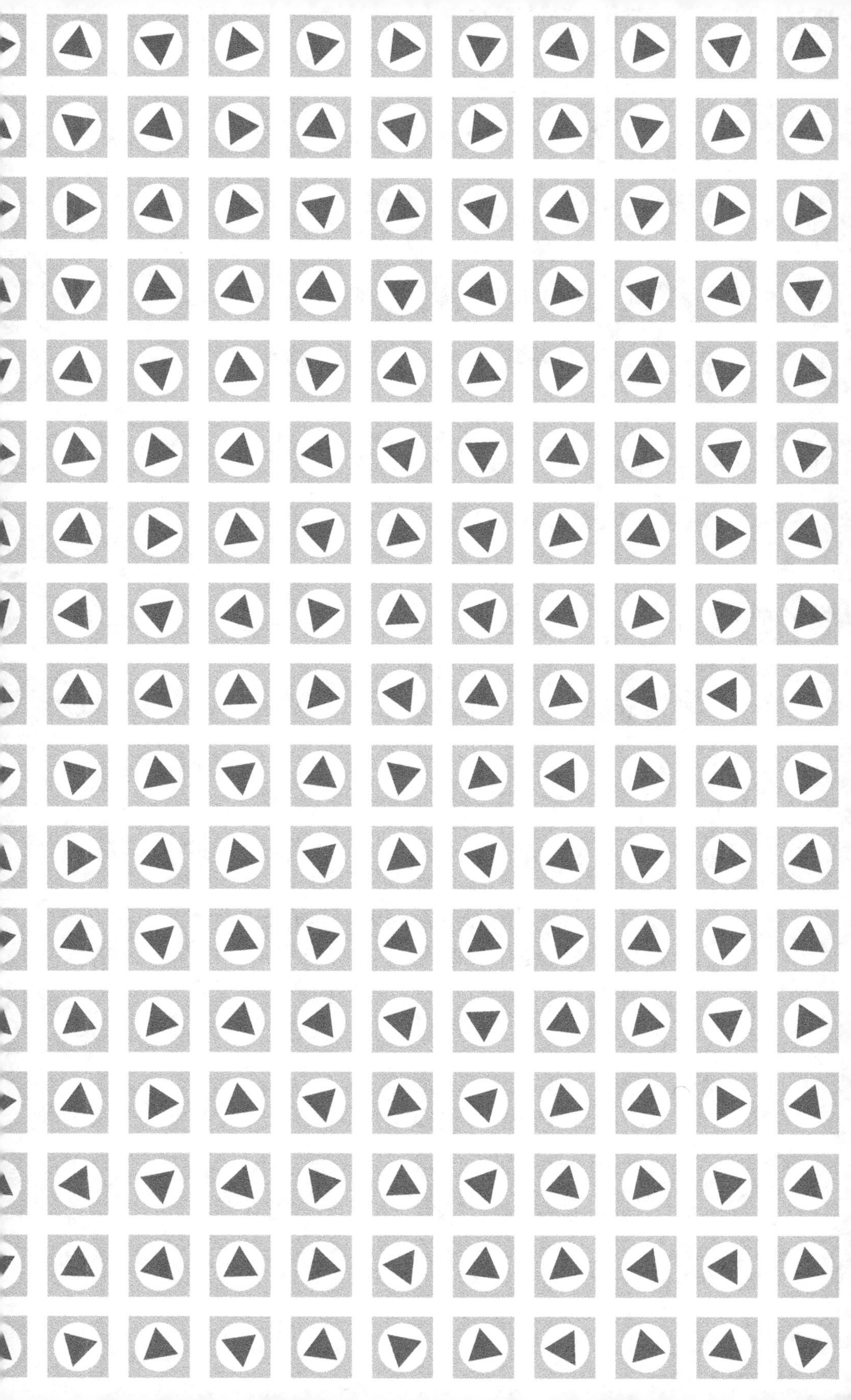

Vision

80% of nonprofits feel they do NOT have a Vision that's propelling them in a positive direction.

2

VISION

Vision has become one of the most overwrought and overwritten topics for leaders in the last twenty years.

Yet many leaders still struggle to articulate a compelling future for their organizations. On the surface, that sounds paradoxical: If so many books, articles, and workshops exist about Vision, why are we still wrestling with it? Well, because statistics tell a sobering truth:

> *Only 20% of nonprofits feel they have a Vision that's propelling them in a positive direction.*

Part of the problem is that a clear and compelling "Vision" can be challenging to land. It can easily become a lofty cliché or an aspirational statement on the office wall, which is well-meaning but not actionable. When Vision is shaped by committee, it tends to get watered down into safe, forgettable language that lacks conviction or is muddied by the perceived need to include everyone's pet project rather than one unified goal. When in survival mode, organizations rarely have space to step back and clarify long-term direction, so Vision gets buried under daily demands.

Patrick Lencioni notes in *The Advantage:* "People crave clarity more than they might admit. When your Vision is muddled, you force team members to guess what success looks like—and that guesswork erodes morale."

Moonshot: A time-bound, measurable, slice of your Vision.

In this chapter, we will take a very different approach to Vision from other sources you may have encountered. We will not spend time helping you create a Vision statement because our assumption is that you have one already. Instead, we will introduce you to the concept of creating a Moonshot: a time-bound, measurable slice of your Vision. The Moonshot will help you accomplish your goal by eliminating guesswork and will become a North Star so clear that everyone can see it and follow it.

Rather than create another generic statement, let's craft something that genuinely drives your organization forward!

Big Vision + Vision Statement + Moonshot = Momentum

Before landing your Moonshot (pun intended), it's essential that we frame the relationship it has with Vision.

Most of us are familiar with Russian nesting dolls, called babushka dolls. They are hollow, hand-painted wooden figures that split horizontally at the middle to reveal another smaller doll inside. That second doll also splits to reveal a third. We see the relationship between Vision and Moonshot this way. Notice the image below that illustrates their connection:

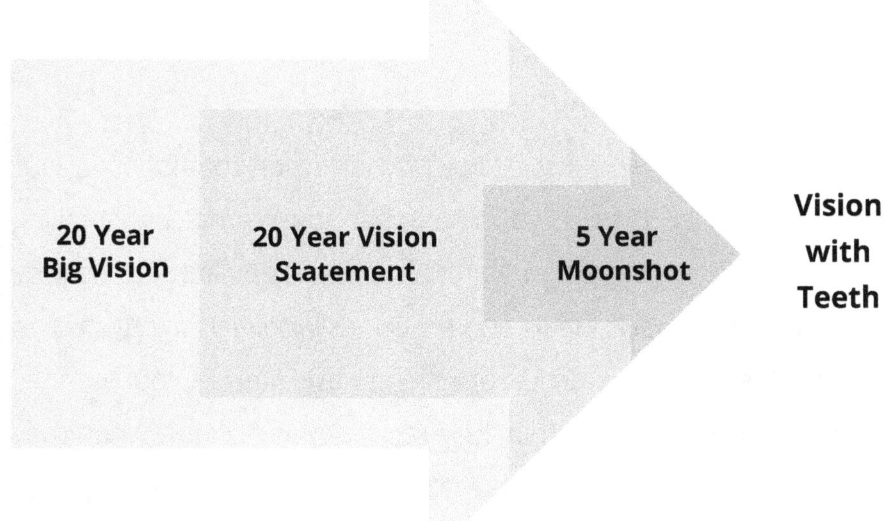

1. Big Arrow – 20 Year Big Vision

Your Big Vision is what makes you jump out of bed, gets you through chaotic staff meetings, and keeps you pushing for impact. At its core, it is "a preferred picture of the future": a sense of what could be if you have the will to pursue it. It is the "why" behind everything you do and the reason you sacrifice so much for a greater cause.

Example: *We see a future in which everyone has a home.*

2. Medium-Sized Arrow – 20 Year Vision Statement

This is the embodiment of your Big Vision in Statement form. It is a big-picture, inspirational, one-sentence rallying cry for staff, volunteers, and donors. It is *meaningful* because it connects everyone to a larger purpose. It is also *memorable* because it is compelling and sticky.

Example: *We exist to create a city knit together by compassion, where everyone has a safe place to sleep and a path toward a better tomorrow.*

3. Smaller Arrow – Moonshot

This is a time-bound, *measurable* slice of your Vision that focuses your nonprofit like a laser. It helps you know that you are not only making progress toward your Big Vision, but it also clarifies what to do next by bridging the gap between ideals and action. As we like to say, "It's Vision with teeth." This is not a reduction of Vision to dry metrics, but it does mean embedding signposts that help teams know not only when they are moving in the right direction but also when they are fulfilling what they intend to do. When a Vision includes indicators of success quantitatively and/or qualitatively, it becomes something everyone can follow.

Example: *By 2030, we will help create a city knit together by compassion, where homelessness is reduced by at least 50%, every individual has access to safe and stable shelter, and clear pathways to long-term housing, employment, and community support is established for all.*

Creating your Moonshot is not about randomly grabbing aspirational measurables and attaching them to your Vision. So, let's take a deeper dive.

The Kennedy Moonshot

One of the most iconic examples of a time-bound slice of Vision in action is President John F. Kennedy's 1961 declaration that the United States would land a man on the Moon and return him safely before the decade was out. The story behind the Moonshot remains one of the most powerful metaphors for us. It has shaped our branding, influenced how we tell stories, and inspired us to write three books exploring its impact.

Dubbed the Moonshot, it was bold, insane-sounding to many, and fully time-bound. "I believe that this nation should commit itself to achieving the goal, before this decade is out, of landing a man on the moon and returning him safely to the earth," Kennedy proclaimed. More than 60 years later, we can't fully grasp how audacious this was. The dream seemed borderline impossible considering the primitive technology by today's standards. Yet it lit a fire under a nation, channeled resources, and galvanized NASA to leap beyond known barriers.

Why was it so potent? It contained three critical factors:

1. **Meaningful:** Achieving this would represent an extraordinary leap in scientific and national progress, serving as a powerful symbol of possibility.

2. **Memorable:** "We're going to the moon!" Everyone could picture the crisp, dramatic, and unambiguous goal in their heads.

3. **Measurable:** "Before this decade is out." There was a ticking clock. No waffle-words like "eventually," or "whenever," or "one day." They had an expiration date, so the dream demanded urgent, innovative steps.

Now, here is what we often forget: Kennedy's BIG VISION was far more expansive than "land a man on the moon." They wanted to explore space, push the boundaries of science, and win the space race. But even bigger than that, the Vision for the United States was to win the ideological battle: USA (democracy) vs. the Soviet Union (communism). If it was going to do that, it needed something to inspire and push people beyond what they thought was possible.

If they could focus on this one Moonshot, this one time-bound slice of the bigger Vision, they could amass an advantage that would not only get us to the Moon faster, but that would aid the larger battle: Win the ideological war.

But the "moon by decade's end" vow gave that broader dream teeth. The Apollo missions harnessed thousands of engineers, scientists, and astronauts, culminating in Neil Armstrong's "giant leap for mankind" in 1969. The Moonshot was...well...the Moon. But the actual Vision? It was defeating the Soviet Union.

That's the function of a Moonshot in your nonprofit. Sure, you want to see an end to homelessness, universal literacy, or a fair economy. But those Visions might be decades away.

A Moonshot is memorable, meaningful, and measurable.

Meanwhile, your staff needs a slice of that grand Vision they can accomplish in the medium term. Something that requires them to stretch, collaborate, and innovate. Translate that spark into a concrete, time-bound challenge that is achievable in five to ten years. That's your Moonshot.

All of this brings us to the description of a Moonshot:

- A Moonshot is a time-bound slice of your Vision.
- It's the arrival at a specific point in your Vision, with a firm completion date.
- Your Moonshot is memorable, meaningful, and measurable.

Across our work with hundreds of nonprofits, we've consistently observed that breaking down a big dream into a single, time-bound slice of their Vision is a game-changer.

Why? Because people crave clarity and a sense of progress. A massive, indefinite dream can grind even the most passionate people down. As more and more time passes, success seems out of reach. But when there's a Moonshot, the Mission stands a stronger chance of commanding resources, unifying staff, and compelling donors.

The Moonshot Tool

Nonprofits don't tend to lack a grand cause. Your Mission began because a group of people deeply cared about changing something fundamental in the world. But ironically, that big dream can become too large, too indefinite. Staff, volunteers, and donors see a horizon so distant that everyday tasks can feel like drops in an ocean. It's hard to be motivated by something day in and day out that feels like it may not happen in your lifetime (or your kids' lifetime).

So it's not about scrapping your Vision; it's about distilling it into something specific enough to unify efforts, like setting out to help 50% of your region's homeless population find stable housing by 2030. It's crisp, bold, and trackable.

Steve Shallenberger in *Becoming Your Best* says, "People are hungry for progress, not just motion." Being busy does not equal progress. A Moonshot ensures progress is visible, fuels morale, attracts donors, and serves as a forcing function that moves strategy from paper to action. It brings urgency to your meetings, direction to your planning, and clarity to every "yes" and "no." It shrinks the gap between Vision and execution. Most of all, it creates a shared win that your people can rally around. It takes something massive and makes it feel possible. After all, how do you eat an elephant? One bite at a time.

The Three Circles of the Moonshot Tool: Deep Passion, Team Expertise, Emerging Opportunity

This tool, adapted from Jim Collins' Hedgehog Concept, transforms Vision from a vague aspiration into a time-bound, strategic slice that is both inspiring and executable.

Other frameworks might generate good ideas, but these three intersecting circles generate alignment, traction, and momentum. We selected the concepts for each of these circles because they surface the essential intersection between moral clarity, core competency, and contextual timing. This combination is uniquely necessary for nonprofit impact.

Unlike businesses, nonprofits don't exist to chase trends or revenue alone; they must root their short-term strategy in what morally compels their team (Deep Passion), what they're exceptionally equipped to do (Team Expertise), and what the world is practically inviting them to do right now (Emerging Opportunity).

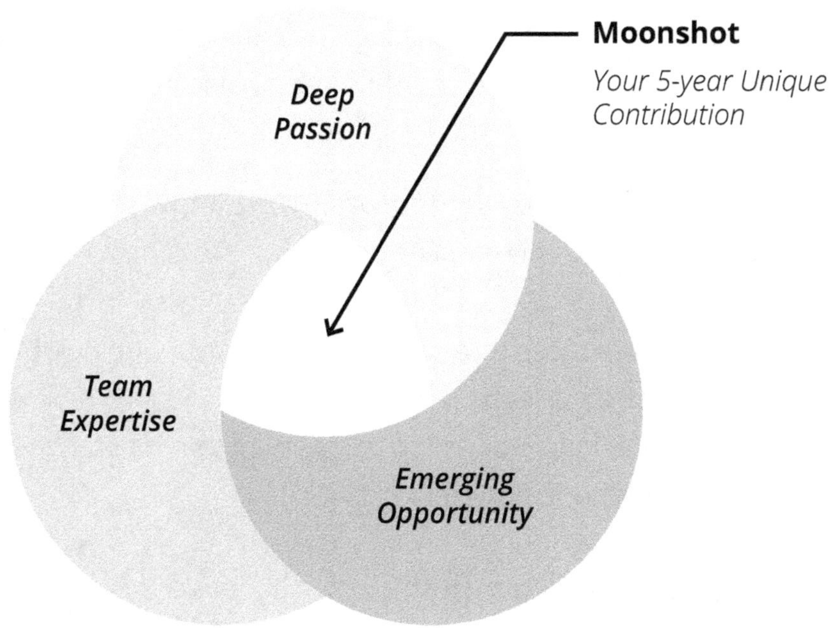

Deep Passion: What ignites your team at a soul level? This is the moral imperative. If your staff leaps out of bed thinking about mental health reform, that's your passion zone.

Core Question: *What gets us up in the morning?*

Team Expertise: Where does your nonprofit truly shine? Maybe your staff excels at grassroots mobilization or data-driven advocacy. Clarity of strengths fosters alignment. Don't attempt a futuristic VR learning platform if your collective skill lies in personal mentorship.

Core Question: *What killer skill sets do we bring to the table?*

Emerging Opportunity: Vision is about the future. Look for the opportunity no one else is adequately addressing, or notice how your community's challenges are shifting. This means being curious and paying attention to both the changing needs in front of you and to the winds at your back. That's when you'll see low-hanging fruit.

Core Question: *What is trying to happen? Where are we seeing unexpected wins, and should we throw gasoline on it?*

Moonshot: Where these three circles overlap is your unique Moonshot – the portion of your Vision you can realistically tackle next. It's large enough to be inspiring, but not so gargantuan that it paralyzes you. It's your next bite of the "Vision elephant."

The Reasonability Factor

It's also essential to employ the reasonability factor when crafting your Moonshot.

A few years ago, a nonprofit declared a Moonshot to eradicate illiteracy across their entire state within 2 years. They had seven full-time employees, a shoestring budget, and zero partnerships. Everyone admired their zeal but saw the meltdown coming: staff burnout, unrealistic funder expectations, and deflated morale. They were missing the circle checks: Did they have the expertise? Could they identify an emerging opportunity to address? Could they begin with a more achievable Moonshot?

Eventually, they recalibrated to a five-year plan, focusing their Moonshot on four pilot districts and turning it into something that had teeth. That pivot reenergized staff and donors because now it felt both meaningful and achievable.

Poetry & Prose: How to Express Your Moonshot

In forging your Moonshot, you need poetry (inspiration) and prose (actionable detail). As Burt Nanus says in *Visionary Leadership*, "A well-conceived Vision speaks to both the heart and the mind." Using the example from above about reducing homelessness, notice how both of these activate something different:

- **Poetry:** captures the heart/emotion.

  Example: Everyone deserves a safe place to sleep and a path toward a better tomorrow.

- **Prose:** aligns the mind.

  Example: By 2030...homelessness is reduced by at least 50%....

- **Poetry & Prose =** By 2030, we will help create a city knit together by compassion, where homelessness is reduced by at least 50%, every individual has access to safe and stable shelter, and clear pathways to long-term housing, employment, and community support is established for all.

The statement needed to include both poetry and prose to make it *memorable*, *meaningful*, and *measurable*.

Risk Ownership

Now, let's say you spend some time working with your team on your Moonshot, but your board is hesitant and may wonder what happens if you fail. Indeed, a big, time-bound target is risky. Yet Michael Hyatt insists, "Vision must be big enough to stretch people but not so gigantic that it feels absurd." You need that sweet spot that demands creativity but remains within plausible grasp.

If you're not risking failure with your Moonshot, you're not shooting for the Moon.

Overcome hesitation by involving stakeholders early from your different spheres of influence: the Leadership Team, staff, donors, volunteers, and board members. Show them the data, highlight your existing strengths, and let them speak into the formation of the Moonshot. This is where Lencioni's "team cohesion" principle thrives: "Vision flourishes in an atmosphere of open communication, accountability, and genuine care." If folks co-create the goal, they'll own its success. If it's handed down from the mountaintop, they might passively resist.

If you're not risking failure with your Moonshot, you're not shooting for the Moon.

Here's why boldly owning your Moonshot is worth the risk:

A local Bright Futures chapter we worked with set a bold goal: reduce teen pregnancy from 12% to 7% in five years.

That clear target unified schools, clinics, and community leaders in a way their previous efforts hadn't. Everyone knew what they were aiming for and by when. By year two, they had already surpassed their goal, hitting 7%. The clarity and urgency of the Moonshot didn't just guide strategy – it galvanized momentum. Funding grew, programs expanded, and volunteers leaned in with fresh energy.

Because the nonprofit had a time-bound, measurable goal, everyone could celebrate a clear victory and push the success further than anyone had initially imagined.

Examples of Strong Moonshots

We want to further illustrate the Moonshot by analyzing examples of three different nonprofit Moonshots:

1. **Housing Nonprofit**

    - **Vision:** End chronic homelessness in Springfield.
    - **Moonshot:** "Within five years, we will reduce chronic homelessness by 40% in our city by securing stable, long-term housing for 600 individuals—combining job-training, mental health resources, and landlord partnerships."
    - **Why It's Good:** It's bold but not outlandish, time-bound, and directly tied to measurable outcomes. Staff see precisely how they contribute: tracking housing placements, forging new landlord alliances, etc.

2. **Education Nonprofit**

    - **Vision:** Every child reading at or above grade level by fourth grade.
    - **Moonshot:** "In the next four years, we will ensure that 80% of third graders in two target school districts meet or exceed

reading benchmarks by using a volunteer reading coach system and a digital literacy program."

- **Why It's Good:** Sharply defined, local focus, four-year horizon. "80% of third graders" is a straightforward metric. Partnerships with reading coaches are feasible, yet demand a stretch.

3. **Environmental Nonprofit**

- **Vision:** Restoring coastal wetlands for ecological balance.
- **Moonshot:** "In five years, we will restore 2,000 acres of damaged wetlands along the Atlantic Coast, planting 1 million native plants and engaging 500 community volunteers."

- **Why It's Good:** The timeline and scope are ambitious but not pie-in-the-sky. The targeted acreage and volunteer engagement figures are unambiguous, giving staff a "north star" for planning.

Examples of Weak Moonshots

For comparison, here are three examples of Moonshots that might look decent on the surface but contain fatal flaws:

1. **Vague and Overreaching**

- **Stated Moonshot:** "We will eliminate hunger in Africa within the next decade."

- **Why It's Weak:** It's far too broad and unrealistic for a single nonprofit, especially within ten years. What this communicates is that they don't understand the depth of the challenge and the obstacles in the way. Staff are set up for disappointment, and donors see a lofty statement without credible methods or scope. There's no sense of how many people are being served or how they're being served.

2. **No Clear Metrics**

    - **Stated Moonshot:** "We will ensure children thrive academically in our region by 2032."
    - **Why It's Weak:** "Thrive academically" is vague. No baseline, no mention of test scores or specific skill sets, no mention of the scope, or how many children. Lacks a truly measurable target. This nonprofit could claim victory without knowing whether they were successful.

3. **Unmotivating Timeframe**

    - **Stated Moonshot:** "Over the next twenty years, we hope to reduce the community's unemployment rates."
    - **Why It's Weak:** Twenty years is too long to feel urgent. "Reduce unemployment" is unspecific, giving no baseline or final target. Staff and donors won't sense the immediacy needed to spark action or creativity

Coaching Tip: Too often, an overly long timeline or vague measures mask the fear of committing to a bold, time-bound goal and fail the test of being memorable, meaningful, and measurable within a plausible timeframe. They either shoot for the stars with zero practicality, or they're so fuzzy no one can rally behind them.

Conclusion

Vision in a nonprofit is more than a statement slapped onto brochures; it's the lifeblood that aligns every effort. But a Vision lacking teeth becomes beige wallpaper, easily overlooked and ultimately meaningless. If you don't define a sharp Vision, donors and daily crises will define your agenda for you.

While the words Vision and Moonshot are not synonymous, they do share significant overlap, which brings clarity. A Moonshot ensures your Vision stays vivid and actionable by giving your team a time-bound target they can truly lock on to that will pull them forward. When that Vision is broken into a near-term, time-bound Moonshot, your staff knows exactly what they must do, donors see precisely where their funds will go, and volunteers become unstoppable ambassadors.

This is your invitation to craft or refresh your own Moonshot. Gather your leadership, look at your passion and expertise, and scan the horizon for emerging needs. Ask: "What do we feel responsible for? How do we want to see change in the next five or ten years? How might we distill our dream into a big challenge that demands both creativity and collaboration?" Then articulate it with enough detail so everyone can see the path. Don't shy away from a risk that offers reward while remaining reasonable.

If you're still hesitant or afraid of failing, consider that your alternative is drifting in perpetual mediocrity, never testing your true potential. A strong Moonshot aligns your community, builds momentum, and creates impact you might never have achieved otherwise. Even if you don't reach 100% of your target, you'll land far closer than if you had never tried at all.

A Moonshot doesn't just clarify – it catalyzes. It aligns your team, energizes your donors, and gives your Vision the urgency it needs to move from aspiration to action. Every meaningful movement begins when a leader dares to say: "Here's where we're going. And here's when we'll get there."

More than sixty years ago, President Kennedy stood before the nation and declared, "We choose to go to the moon, not because it is easy, but because it is hard." He knew that bold, time-bound challenges have the power to focus people, ignite innovation, and bend history.

That's what your Moonshot can do.

Not because your mission is easy. But because it's worth everything you've got.

Set it. Say it. Own it.

And let your Moonshot move the Mission forward!

Vision

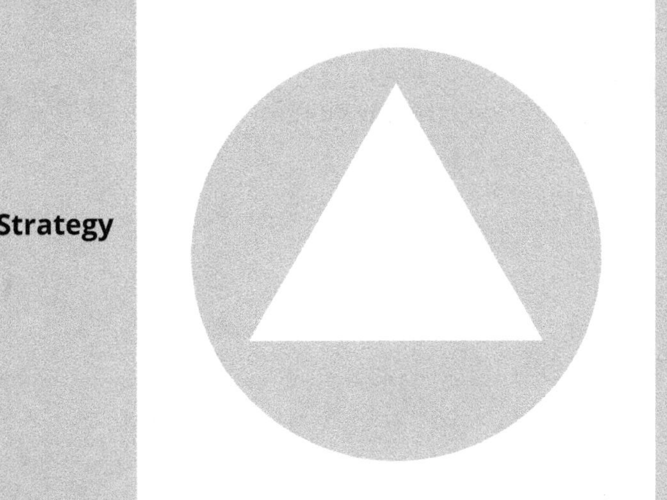

86% of nonprofits with a clear strategy experience increased results.

3

STRATEGY

If strategy is how you get from Point A (where you are now) to Point B (where you want to be in the future), how do you develop a winning strategy that directs the appropriate amount of time, money, and passion toward accomplishing your goals?

Richard Rumelt is probably the best living strategist in the world and wrote the definitive book on strategy, *Good Strategy/Bad Strategy*. In this book, he argues, "Strategy is not mere ambition; it's a cohesive response to a critical challenge." In a nonprofit context, your "critical challenge" might be alleviating homelessness or improving educational outcomes for underprivileged youth. The difference is that big-hearted intentions rarely translate into big-hearted impact without deliberate planning built on a winning strategy.

Traditional strategic planning is designed for businesses, not for nonprofits and mission-driven organizations like yours. The Impact Operating System, on the other hand, was created for and refined by nonprofits.

So, in this chapter, we want to look at two big questions:

1. What is a winning strategy?
2. How do you create a winning strategy and get it on the road?

What Is a Winning Strategy?

Strategist Mark Pollard says, "Strategy is an informed opinion about how to win." "Win", in your context, refers to achieving meaningful impact. It's not about outcompeting other charities for donations; it's about overcoming challenges such as illiteracy, hunger, or environmental degradation.

Winning means seeing real outcomes that align with your mission and moving steadily toward the future you dreamed of. Winning is beating back the injustices of this world.

Said another way, the goal is not to have a strategy. The goal is to have a winning strategy that works in real life, guiding you from your current reality (Point A) to your bold, transformative destination (Point B), your Moonshot.

The goal is not to have a strategy. The goal is to have a winning strategy that works in real life.

Where Nonprofits Get Tripped Up

Strategy is about making the right choices: knowing where to focus, what to ignore, and how to allocate resources to stand a genuine chance at hitting your Moonshot.

Nonprofits often confuse planning with strategy. Planning is the list of tactics, like the nuts-and-bolts of change management; strategy is the driving logic behind them. If you treat your entire strategy as a to-do list, you will miss the nuance that gives it power. Strategy is your filter for decisions on what you will and will not do. It's your high-level lens for deciding how to turn an inspiring vision into tangible results on the ground.

But not all strategies are created equal.

Nonprofits often confuse planning with strategy.

In fact, there are hallmarks of BAD strategy. Things like: 1) Fluffy cotton candy statements that sound like corporate jargon, 2) Mistaking setting a goal for a strategy (this is the most common mistake), or 3) A strategy that doesn't seem to understand its most significant obstacles. It's crucial to wrestle those things to the ground if you want to create a winning strategy.

How Do You Create a Winning Strategy and Get It On the Road?

Step #1: Define Your Moonshot

In the previous chapter, we introduced the concept of the Moonshot: "Land a man on the moon and return him safely within the decade." The Moonshot is a time-bound, measurable slice of your Big Vision.

Your Moonshot represents Point B – the clear destination your strategy should be guiding you toward. Unless you define "winning" concretely, you cannot strategize effectively.

Step #1:

Define Your Moonshot

Step #2: Name the Obstacles

Let's be blunt: Nonprofits tend to shy away from naming challenging issues, or they don't spend enough time truly understanding the complexities and the barriers they represent. Maybe you fear donors will see you as incompetent. Or perhaps you don't want to rock the boat with staff. But if you can't name the rocky conditions, your plan will shatter.

So, the second step is to assess the most significant obstacles you are facing that will prevent you from achieving your Moonshot. They tend to be different for each nonprofit, but here are some examples:

- High donor churn
- Staff burnout

- Difficulty reaching the client population because the bus routes shifted
- Outdated digital platforms
- Not enough people know we exist

Jot some of your obstacles down, unvarnished, and stare them in the face. This is crucial because real strategy emerges from solving real problems. You can't solve what you're too nervous to name. In fact, avoidance or denial ensures the problem wins by default.

Many nonprofits think a bold mission statement or compelling heart story can override any deficit. But that's not enough. Even a Moonshot alone falls short. You need to clearly articulate your challenges and address them directly for your time-bound, measurable goal to be achievable.

Step #3: Formulate an Impact Strategy

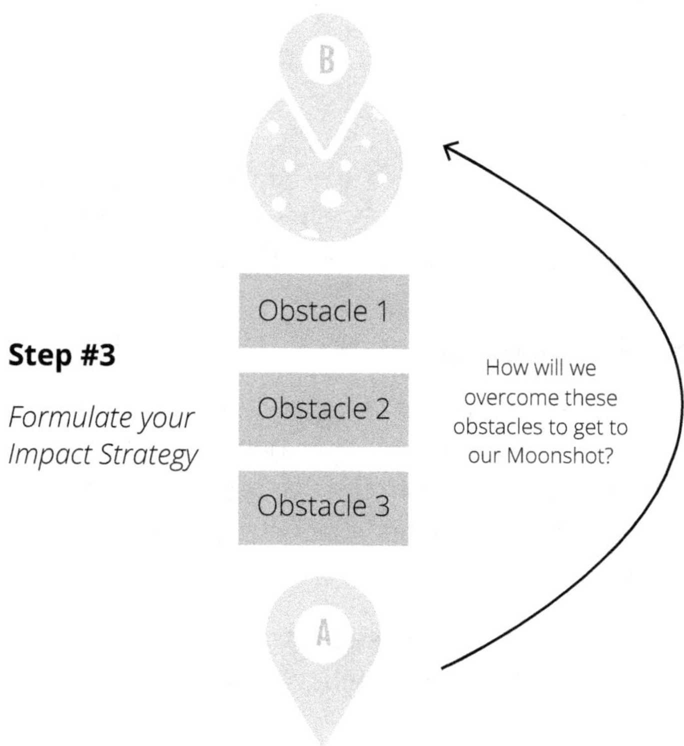

After you have created your Moonshot and named your Obstacles, the next step is to create an Impact Strategy. But how do you go about creating this? Richard Rumelt suggests that a winning strategy contains a hypothesis. We call this hypothesis an *IF / THEN strategy statement*:

> "*IF* we focus on X approach,
> *THEN* we believe Y impact will follow."

The formula looks like this:

> X = winning strategy
>
> Y = the destination - Point B (achieving your Moonshot)

Simply stating that you want to raise more funds is not articulating a strategy. That is a goal. Many nonprofits confuse goals and strategy. Real strategy connects a means to an end. It's an educated guess at how to win, given your constraints and resources.

Example: Rise

Before moving on to Step 4, let's take a quick look at an example. Rise is a nonprofit that helps teen moms in a midwestern mid-major city. Here is how they navigated Steps 1-3 in building their Impact Strategy:

1. Rise Defined Their Moonshot

Rise's Big Vision is to help teen moms avoid getting trapped in a system of poverty, unable to provide for their babies, and living in substandard housing. So they wrestled with the question, "What does success look like?" After multiple leadership meetings and listening sessions with program participants, they arrived at a clear Moonshot:

> Within five years, 80% of teen moms who enter our program will graduate from high school and enroll in college or a career-track job.

It was meaningful. It was memorable. It was measurable. That clarity transformed conversations across the organization because it aligned energy and resources around helping them complete their secondary education. This, in turn, increased their opportunities for gainful employment.

2. Rise Named the Obstacles

They held a half-day offsite and asked the team, "What prevents our moms from graduating?" Here's a list of a few of the biggest obstacles they came up with:

- Transportation gaps that made it hard to get to school or child care
- Emotional trauma without adequate mental health support
- Irregular school attendance due to a lack of structure

- Lack of stable housing
- Limited relationships with employers post-graduation

After naming these obstacles, they were ready to create their impact strategy.

3. Rise Formulated an Impact Strategy

Here are some Impact Strategy examples that Rise explored, but ultimately decided would not be a winning strategy:

- IF we expand into multiple cities within 3 years, THEN we will increase the number of teen moms we serve by 300%.

  *Why they did not choose this: This strategy prioritized growth over depth. It sounded ambitious, but they hadn't yet solved core issues at their current site, such as retention, program consistency, or staffing. Scaling without solving was a recipe for collapse.

- IF we invest in an aggressive digital awareness campaign, THEN we will attract more donors and double our budget.

  *Why they did not choose this: Fundraising mattered, but their most significant issue was infrastructure, not visibility. More money would not be beneficial if they did not have strong service delivery, staff clarity, and measurable outcomes. Donors are more likely to give if they see a clear theory of change, not just clever marketing.

- IF we create a mentorship app to connect alum moms with current participants, THEN we will improve retention and outcomes through peer support.

> *Why they did not choose this: This innovative option sounds very attractive. However, their teen moms were overwhelmed with just managing daily life. Adding technical complexity did not address their most urgent needs, such as childcare, transportation, and academic coaching. It was a good supplementary idea, but not a core strategy.

Each of these tempting directions carried potential value. Still, Rise ultimately chose a strategy that was more grounded, evidence-informed, and directly responsive to the real barriers their participants were facing. Naming the barriers in Step 2 helped them build a winning strategy:

> IF we provide holistic wraparound services that include stable housing, on-site childcare, academic coaching, and career mentorship, THEN at least 80% of teen moms will graduate and transition to a job or college.

Once this clarity landed and they embraced it together, this Impact Strategy became the backbone of all their decisions and programming. Now they needed to get it on the road.

Step #4: Build Your Impact Roadmap

Now that you have created your Impact Strategy Statement, it's time to build your Impact Roadmap with accompanying tactics.

The Impact Roadmap Tool helps you bring your Moonshot all the way down to daily execution. It draws on proven frameworks and tools from leading thinkers, including the Rockefeller Habits, the Patterson Center's StratOp process, Auxano's Vision Framing, the Vision/Traction Organizer (V/TO), cascading communications models, the Balanced Scorecard, Objectives and Key Results (OKRs), and others. Over the years, we have refined this tool and adapted it to focus on impact rather than revenue.

Impact Strategy Statement

This sits at the top of the Roadmap and serves as your compass. It's a concise expression of your hypothesis. Remember Rise's example: "IF we provide wraparound services that include stable housing, on-site childcare, academic coaching, and career mentorship, THEN at least 80% of teen moms will graduate and transition to a job or college."

Four 3-Year Milestones

These milestones reflect the key strategic moves you believe will bring you closer to your vision in three years.

There are three components for each milestone:

- **Categories:**

  These are the organizing principles for each Milestone, such as Fundraising, Program Innovation, Community Partnerships, etc. Determine the categories that are most important for making progress, and know you are on your way to achieving your 5-year Moonshot.

- **Key Performance Indicators (KPI):**

  KPIs turn strategy into numbers that an organization can track and act on. Maybe your housing center KPI is a 70% client retention rate in stable housing after six months. Maybe your volunteer program KPI is a 90% volunteer satisfaction rate. Clear, measurable indicators answer the question, "What does success look like for each milestone?"

- **Articulations:**

  Articulate what success means in each category. For example, Fundraising: "Forming and activating a four-person development team with clear annual fundraising targets." Or, Program Innovation: "Implementing digital literacy modules that improve client skill levels by at least one proficiency band within six months."

Here's how Rise formulated their 3-Year Milestones:

1. Housing: Open and operate a second residential site to serve 20 additional teen moms annually.
2. Childcare: Build licensed, extended-hour childcare at both campuses.
3. Academic Support: Hire a team of academic coaches at a 1:10 ratio to provide tailored educational support.
4. Career Pathways: Develop five formal partnerships with local employers offering job training or internships.

Here's how their Moonshot and 3-Year Milestones map onto the Impact Roadmap framework:

5 Year

Impact Strategy

IF we provide wraparound services that include stable housing, on-site childcare, academic coaching, and career mentorship, THEN at least 80% of teens moms will graduate and transition to a job or college.

3 Year

Housing	Childcare	Academic Coaching	Career Pathways
Open and operate a second residential site to serve 20 additional teen moms annually.	Build licensed, extended-hour childcare at both campuses.	Hire a team of academic coaches with a 1:10 ratio, offering tailored educational support.	Develop five formal partnerships with local employers offering job training or internships.

1-Year Must Win

Organizations often begin their year by naming a laundry list of "good objectives" they intend to chase. This inevitably dilutes focus. The Impact Roadmap takes a different approach: choose one primary objective that must be true in 12 months, is not true today, yet is so critical that achieving it would be a true game-changer.

It does NOT mean that you aren't taking ground in other areas. You certainly will be. However, by identifying your most important win of the year, you're going to make sure it gets a disproportionate amount of time and energy. Why? Because not all wins are created equal.

This "Must Win" could be something like "Recruit and train 100 new volunteers by December" or "Secure a $200,000 matching grant by Q3." It unifies the entire team around a single, organizing principle that everyone can rally behind and accelerates everything else.

Knock down this domino, and many more will follow. The 1-Year Must Win will consistently deliver a disproportionate amount of return. Here is Rise's 1-Year Must Win:

> Secure $350,000 in multi-year funding to launch and fully staff the academic coaching program.

This goal mattered because their data showed that academic engagement was the top lever for long-term success. Winning here made every other Milestone more achievable.

There's nothing worse than feeling like you have an inflexible strategic plan that was built for a world that no longer exists.

Four 90-Day Goals

90-Day Goals are quarterly sprints that correspond to the 3-year Milestones directly above it.

These shorter goals keep you agile. In 90 days, you can see if your strategy is working or if you need to adjust. There's nothing worse than feeling like you have an inflexible strategic plan that was built for a world that no longer exists.

For Rise, these 90-Day Goals completed the puzzle of their Impact Roadmap, connecting their Impact Strategy and their 3-Year Milestones:

1. Housing: Complete feasibility and zoning studies for a second housing site.
2. Childcare: Apply for childcare licensure and recruit two lead teachers.
3. Academic Coaching: Finalize job descriptions and hire the first academic coach.
4. Career Pathways: Host an employer roundtable and secure MOUs from two anchor job partners.

Here is Rise's completed Impact Roadmap:

5 Year — Outcome

Impact Strategy

IF we provide wraparound services that include stable housing, on-site childcare, academic coaching, and career mentorship, THEN at least 80% of teens moms will graduate and transition to a job or college.

3 Year — Milestones

Housing	Childcare	Academic Coaching	Career Pathways
Open and operate a second residential site to serve 20 additional teen moms annually.	Build licensed, extended-hour childcare at both campuses.	Hire a team of academic coaches with a 1:10 ratio, offering tailored educational support.	Develop five formal partnerships with local employers offering job training or internships.

1 Year — Objective

Secure $350,000 in multi-year funding so we can launch and fully staff the academic coaching program.

90 Days — Goals

Housing	Childcare	Academic Coaching	Career Pathways
Complete feasibility and zoning studies for second housing site.	Apply for childcare licensure and recruit two lead teachers.	Finalize job descriptions and hire the first academic coach.	Host an employer roundtable and secure MOUs from two anchor job partners.

How to Make Sure Your Plan Remains Razor-Sharp

- Every three years, refresh your milestones.
- Every year, refresh your 1-Year Objectives.
- Every quarter, refresh your 90-Day Goals.

This is what allows you to be flexible and nimble, factoring in what you are learning as you adapt to changes in your organization, city, and broader culture. The Impact Roadmap is not a rigid, linear plan, but a dynamic tool for clarity, experimentation, and movement.

Impact Roadmap Coaching Tips

1. Provide Impact Roadmap Training for Your Staff

If your staff or volunteers are not accustomed to accountability frameworks, it may take time for them to adopt the process. Provide training or run a pilot for a few months. Force-feeding a Roadmap rarely works.

2. Assign Ownership

Assign owners for each 90-day goal. Clarity in accountability ensures people know who to contact with updates or challenges.

3. Celebrate Wins

Strategy can feel like a grind if you are constantly chasing the next target. Acknowledge milestones you've hit, whether you gather the team, ring a bell, or send a celebratory email. Do something that celebrates progress! This fosters motivation and loyalty.

4. Incorporate a Weekly Component

One reason the Impact Roadmap works so well is that it doesn't stop at the 90-Day Goals; it drills down to practical, weekly actions for every staff member. Rather than introducing this to you here, we will do so in Chapter 8: People and Chapter 10: Rhythms, because it reveals how it helps every team member focus like a heat-seeking missile.

5. Adapt as You Learn

No matter how brilliant your initial strategy, unexpected changes such as funding cuts, global events, and staff transitions will test it. Flexibility is key to avoiding prolonged, draining battles. If your approach does not meet expectations and you have had enough time to adequately test your hypothesis, pivot into what you have learned rather than stubbornly doubling down. The Impact Roadmap and the rhythms that accompany it were designed with this in mind.

Conclusion

A cohesive, winning strategy is not about impressing donors with polished slide decks or a thick binder that you'll never open again. It is about achieving tangible impact through a system that ensures clarity, alignment, and consistent execution. That's precisely what the Impact Operating System offers: a structured way for you to lead, manage, and deliver high-impact outcomes. Instead of allowing big visions and lofty goals to die on the vine, your customized ImpactOS ties all the components—Vision, Strategy, Development, Metrics, Culture, People, Systems, and Rhythms—into a framework that keeps you focused, nimble, and highly impactful.

Donors appreciate this clarity just as much as you do. They are more confident investing when they see a practical roadmap used to drive the mission forward.

Volunteers feel energized by an actionable strategy that makes them partners in the mission, rather than cogs in a machine.

Staff will pull in unison, like a well-coordinated rowing crew.

Communities you serve will recognize your credibility when they see consistent, trackable progress, not just good intentions. When someone asks about your vision and strategy, you will point to real work already in motion. You'll show how the Roadmap you are following clarifies your focus and prioritizes your energy to achieve real impact.

You can break the cycle of glossy strategic plans that gather dust or seem empty as they hang on a wall. The Impact Operating System turns your strategy into a living, breathing process that is revisited, adapted, and strengthened by what you are learning on the ground every day.

30% of nonprofits will shut down in the next decade due to financial instability.

4

DEVELOPMENT

In the summer of 2014, the ALS Ice Bucket Challenge took the world by storm. What started as a grassroots awareness campaign quickly snowballed into a viral movement. With just a bucket of ice water, a smartphone, and a social media tag, people across the globe were soaking themselves to support the cause. In just eight weeks, the ALS Association raised over $115 million, a staggering leap from the $2.8 million raised during the same period the year before. The challenge was simple, emotional, wildly shareable, and—most importantly—anchored to a credible organization that already had relationships, infrastructure, and a clear mission.

Naturally, every nonprofit watching thought, "How do we get one of those? If it worked for them, surely it will work for us!" In the years that followed, hundreds of organizations attempted to manufacture their own viral campaigns—'Dunk Tank Challenges,' 'Hot Sauce Challenges,' 'Pajamas for a Cause'—most of which barely worked or straight-up failed.Why didn't they work? Well, because the ALS Association had spent years building a trustworthy brand and strong networks. Without that scaffolding, the splashy stunt would have fallen flat.

Every nonprofit has what Jerold Panas calls "a moral imperative" to raise support for their organization. We agree. But here is a sobering reality:

> *30% of nonprofits will shut their doors over the next decade due to financial instability.*

Leaders like you see what could be a different, better world, *but it takes funding to fuel that vision*. So, you live under constant pressure to meet the bottom line. This can rob you of sleep, drain your energy, and stifle your creativity. It can create a pit in your stomach as you feel the anxiety creeping more and more into your work life (and sometimes your home life).

The moral imperative to raise support does not require finding the latest and greatest silver bullet methodology to solve the pain point. It does, however, require focused, hard work that aligns with your needs and capacity.

In the Impact Operating System, Development is just one crucial piece among Vision, Strategy, Metrics, Culture, People, Systems, and Execution. None of these can exist in isolation. You have already read chapters on Vision and Strategy, discovering how a toothless Vision leads to underwhelming results. The same holds for fundraising: no matter how fancy your appeals, if your Moonshot is flimsy, the strategy appears paper-thin, or your internal processes are chaotic, you will struggle to raise real, sustainable support.

The good news? You can replace the sometimes paralyzing anxiety of fundraising with proactive confidence. We will give you The Sustainable Development Formula, which introduces a simple yet powerful tool: the FUEL Matrix. This tool will help you customize your Development practice for your unique circumstances.

Earlier in this book, we shared that you can think about the Impact Operating System as a rotary engine: multiple parts working in sync to drive your nonprofit forward. Money, quite simply, is the fuel that keeps the engine humming.

In this chapter, we will cover:

- The Two Development Ditches
- The Sustainable Development Formula
- Right-sized Bandwidth, Updated Playbook & Rhythmic Triggers
- The FUEL Matrix Tool

The Two Development Ditches: Bandwidth & Playbook

Raise your hand if you've ever said, "We need a whole new fundraising strategy," immediately after a disappointing campaign. Now, raise your hand if six months later, you were back to planning another version of last year's gala because you couldn't pull off the new strategy you were convinced would work. (We see those hands.)

No shame here. Just a reality check about the fact that, when it comes to Development, there are two ditches that leaders tend to fall into:

1. **The Playbook Ditch (Lack of Innovation):** Are your fundraising methods old, stale, and lackluster, or are they modern, effective, and tailored to your current context?

2. **The Bandwidth Ditch (Lack of Capacity):** Do you have enough energy, digital firepower, and people with time, and are they equipped with the skills needed for the task?

Here's how this could play out (and maybe you've had a similar experience): One day, your board decides you need an audacious new event to attract younger donors—but your tiny staff barely has time to run the annual gala. The next day, you choose to double your major gifts efforts but realize you have never cultivated relationships with wealthy supporters. This "non-virtuous cycle" jerks you back and forth between overextending staff and under-innovating. Everyone ends up exhausted and frustrated, leading to whiplash and uncertain performance.

Do you find yourself vacillating between these ditches? Do you find yourself stuck in one of them currently?

Don't give up... keep reading...there's hope.

The Sustainable Development Formula

Many nonprofit leaders assume their development challenges are tactical: "We need better events," "We need more major donors," "We need a new CRM." But these are surface-level expressions of a deeper issue: a lack of strategic infrastructure that allows Development to scale sustainably.

In other words, the problem isn't just fundraising execution—it's development architecture.

What's often missing isn't effort, passion, or intention, but a cohesive, repeatable system that aligns human capacity, modern strategy, and organizational rhythm to support the long-term mission. It is not a formula for raising emergency funds this quarter, but for building a development system that works over time.

Here's the formula:

Sustainable Development = Right-Sized Bandwidth + Updated Playbook + Rhythmic Refresh

The formula is simple:

- *Bandwidth* ensures you have a stable foundation of people and skill resources.
- *Playbook* ensures you are using relevant, high-ROI tactics aligned with your mission and staff capacity.
- *Rhythmic Refresh* ensures you periodically refresh your approach to Development by staying current rather than sliding into stagnation.

It's deceptively simple, but it's based on the hard-won insight that long-term success isn't about brilliance; it's about structure.

This framework doesn't just help you raise funds, it enables you to understand why so many well-meaning development plans collapse, and how to build one that endures.

Sustainable Development = Right-Sized Bandwidth + Updated Playbook + Rhythmic Refresh

Let's look at each of the three factors in the formula.

Right-Sized Bandwidth

The first factor in the Sustainable Development Formula is Bandwidth. It is, by all accounts, the all-too-often overlooked side of fundraising success. If no one on your team has the time or skillset to execute your brilliant idea, it doesn't matter how impressive it sounds. You will stall out before you ever get off the ground.

Critical Bandwidth Questions

To diagnose your staff bandwidth for Development, answer the following questions, calculate your score, and analyze your results:

Step #1: Answer the Questions

1. How many full-time employees (FTEs) are dedicated to Development?

   If your entire Development team is one overworked manager who also runs programs and HR, *your growth potential is limited.* A single staffer cannot possibly manage major gifts, grants, events, and digital campaigns simultaneously.

   Rate your Bandwidth for staff capacity on a scale of 1 to 10:

   ____

2. What is the role of the Founder or Executive Director/CEO?

   Some leaders are "fundraisers in chief," adept at building relationships. Others are more operationally minded. Clarifying how your top leader fits into the fundraising mix can help you leverage their strengths effectively or decide whether you need more specialized personnel.

   Rate the Bandwidth for your ED/CEO on a scale of 1 to 10:

   ____

3. How many people-hours do we spend each week on Development?

   It's not just about FTEs, but also the quality of time. Are these hours constantly interrupted? Do staff get the chance to build donor relationships, or are they drowning in administrative tasks?

   Rate the Bandwidth for hours needed on a scale of 1 to 10:

   ____

4. What is our team's level of expertise and sophistication?

   Enthusiasm is fantastic, but if no one has ever run a major gift campaign or orchestrated a digital ad funnel, you may need external coaching and consulting because you may need someone who knows how to run those processes.

   Rate the Bandwidth for the team skillset on a scale of 1 to 10:

   ____

5. Is our team committed to continuous learning?

   Fundraising evolves quickly. Those who adopt a "We've always done it this way" mentality risk obsolescence...and fast. If your team is open to trying new methods and is eager for professional Development, you are more likely to adapt and thrive.

   Rate the Bandwidth for continued team development on a scale of 1 to 10:

   ____

6. What is our board's involvement?

   Whatever type of board you have, you want them to be engaged in fundraising in a way that makes sense for what you are asking of them. If you can activate your board, you effectively increase your capacity without increasing payroll.

   Rate the Bandwidth for Board fundraising on a scale of 1 to 10:

   ____

7. What is the culture around Development in our organization?

   Does the staff resent fundraising because they view it as "begging," or do they see it as a shared responsibility to fuel the mission?

   Are they afraid of it or excited by making the ask? It should be no surprise that staff attitudes toward fundraising directly shape how donors perceive the organization's mission.

   Rate your Bandwidth for team attitude on a scale of 1 to 10:

   ____

Step #2: Calculate Your Score

Add your ratings for each of the 7 Bandwidth Questions, and then divide by 7 to get your average.

Write your average here:___________

Step #3: Analyze Your Results

What do your answers to these questions and your score tell you about the state of Development in your organization?

Two Bandwidth Examples

Example #1: Let's say your organization aims to raise $2 million a year. Currently, you have a half-time development coordinator (let's call him Sam) who also manages communications. Sam is bright and committed, but has no training, experience, or expertise in leading major gift strategies or cultivating relationships with high-net-worth prospects. You can attempt the best new campaign you want, but Sam's day is maxed out writing newsletters and juggling board reports. In Sam's situation, the Bandwidth issue was that he didn't have enough time in his week.

Example #2: Your development director (let's call her Sally) quietly jokes, "I'm the Chief Plate Spinner." She even posts videos on Instagram of herself trying to spin actual plates. Grants are Sally's first plate, annual appeals her second, events her third, corporate sponsorship her fourth, volunteer management her fifth, and the list goes on. Eventually, the plates crash. It's simply too many responsibilities for one person to juggle. In her situation, the Bandwidth issue is time.

It's not enough to realize you have a Bandwidth challenge. The real question is: what kind of challenge are you facing? For some nonprofits, the issue is simply too few people. For others, the problem is that existing staff need better training, clearer priorities, or more time set aside to focus on Development.

As fundraising expert Jerold Panas reminds us in *Born to Raise:* "You earn the right to ask (for a donation) by being present, informed, and dedicated long before you schedule an official meeting." In other words, Development isn't just about making the ask. It's about the time and attention you invest in building relationships well before that moment. If your team doesn't have enough time to be genuinely present and informed with donors, your fundraising potential will always be capped.

Right-sized Bandwidth is about ensuring you can fully execute the methods you choose, without burning people out or letting tasks fall through the cracks.

Updated Playbook

The second factor in the Sustainable Development Formula (*Right-Sized Bandwidth + Modern Playbook + Rhythmic Refresh*) is an Updated Playbook. This includes the methods, campaigns, and tactics used to raise funds. For many nonprofits, their fundraising methods are cobbled together from tactics that worked 30+ years ago or cherry-picked from conference success stories. The result is a hodgepodge that doesn't reflect a coherent strategy: that 1990s gala, a random direct mail template discovered a decade ago, or a social media campaign borrowed from a friend's organization. It's no wonder results can be inconsistent.

The 101, 201, 301, 401 Concept

Think of building your Development Playbook like learning a new language. If you skip the basics—greetings, conjugations, simple verbs, essential vocabulary—and jump to advanced conversational speech, you'll soon realize you are lost. Only after you master the basics can you move to intermediate grammar and eventually complex literature. Skip the basics, and you will struggle.

Suppose your fundraising approach tries to jump straight into advanced tactics without a solid base. In that case, you will soon be speaking gibberish, leaving donors confused, uninterested, and they will give somewhere else (or not at all). In other words, don't expect to launch a flashy online peer-to-peer campaign until you have nailed the fundamentals first.

Here's how the logic applies to your fundraising approach:

- 101 is about Foundational Tactics
- 201 helps Intermediate Tactics
- 301 is Advanced Tactics
- 401 requires High Sophistication

The "Big Idea" when it comes to the Playbook: Many nonprofits dabble across these levels, but the results are inconsistent. Before you dive into a flashy new fundraising idea, make sure you master the 101 level first.

The Fuel Matrix Tool

In the Impact Operating System, we developed the FUEL Matrix Tool to help nonprofits build an updated development playbook. The tool systematically evaluates fundraising across nine verticals:

1. **Operations:** Your internal systems, policies, and workflows that support Development.
2. **Technology:** The platforms, CRMs, and communication tools you use.
3. **Data & Insights:** The information you collect, analyze, and apply to guide decisions and measure impact.
4. **Relationships:** Donor stewardship, engagement, and community building practices.
5. **Campaigns:** Specific fundraising initiatives, such as events, peer-to-peer fundraising, major gifts, and recurring giving.
6. **Education:** Training your staff, board, and volunteers in fundraising best practices.
7. **Storytelling:** Crafting narratives that connect donors to your mission and impact.
8. **Thank-You Culture:** The practices that ensure donors feel appreciated and valued beyond the transaction.
9. **Alternative Revenue:** Funding streams beyond traditional donations, such as earned income, partnerships, or grants.

	Operations	Technology	Data & Insights	Relation-ships	Campaigns	Education	Storytelling	Thank You Culture	Alternative Revenue
101 Tactics									
201 Tactics									
301 Tactics									
401 Tactics									

This is the framework for the FUEL Matrix. To protect the integrity of the process, the specific tactics in each section are shared only with organizations participating in the ImpactOS Integration Process outlined in Chapter 11. The remainder of this chapter will double-click on one of the verticals.

Within each vertical, you start at the 101-level and move upward (201, 301, 401). Beware of chasing every shiny new method. Master the basics, then thoughtfully add complexity. This ensures your updated Playbook evolves, not lurches, from one fad to another.

Notice the tactical progression in the Relationships example as seen in the image on the next page:

101: Regular Schedule of Donor Meetings

At the foundational level, this stage involves intentional, face-to-face (or virtual) relationship cultivation. Organizations create a rhythm of check-ins with key donors, listening to their feedback, sharing progress, and deepening alignment between the donor's passions and the nonprofit's mission.

201: Regular Meetings with High-Capacity Donors

At this level, meetings are fewer but more intentional and tailored. You establish a personalized cadence with a small group of high-capacity donors, bring them behind the curtain on vision and priorities, invite honest input, and align their passions with the next most meaningful step forward.

301: Peer-to-Peer Cultivation Via Connectors and Advocates

At this level, relationships multiply through trusted voices. Instead of the organization doing all the cultivating, you equip a small group of connectors and advocates to open doors, host simple touchpoints, and make warm introductions within their networks. The nonprofit stays close to the relationship, but the credibility comes peer-to-peer - creating momentum and trust that staff outreach alone cannot.

401: Training and Deploying Ambassadors

The most advanced strategy empowers others to help carry the mission forward. Nonprofits identify and equip donor champions, or "ambassadors," who can host events, share their giving stories, and introduce new supporters. This tactic multiplies impact through relational influence and peer-to-peer trust, as "Ambassadors" have access to relational networks that development offices do not.

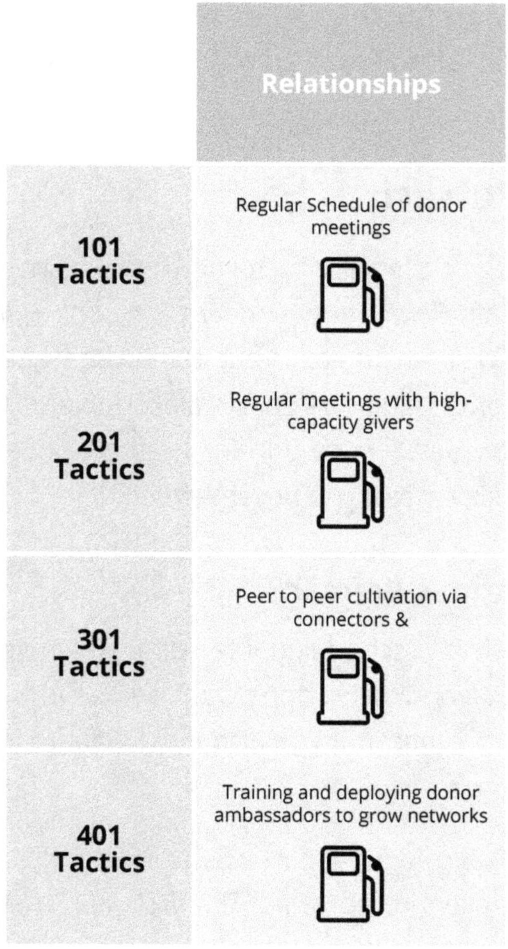

When facilitating a FUEL Matrix workshop with an organization we worked with, a board member kept insisting they try a complex cryptocurrency fundraising campaign. Meanwhile, their donor database was a messy Google spreadsheet maintained by a half-time intern. They were not up to date on donor tracking, writing thank-you notes, or sending impact reports. But they were convinced the only thing missing was this crypto play. We had a good discussion and gently asked them, "What if you mastered the ABCs first and then tackled more complex options like cryptocurrency?" They agreed.

The takeaway? Always match your tactics to your real capacity and donor context. It's the surest way to avoid burnout and wasted effort.

Rhythmic Refresh

We've now arrived at the third factor in the Sustainable Development Formula (*Right-Sized Bandwidth + Modern Playbook + Rhythmic Refresh*). No matter how well you match your Bandwidth and Playbook, time erodes tactics. Donor behaviors shift, staff turnover disrupts continuity, and technology evolves. A once-brilliant strategy with some killer tactics will decay into irrelevance if you never refresh it.

What Is a Rhythmic Refresh?

A rhythmic refresh is a scheduled interval at which you reassess your Bandwidth and Playbook. You don't want a knee-jerk monthly revamp because that's too frantic, but you also don't want to let five years pass without reexamination.

About ten years ago, a nonprofit we worked with scheduled a big "strategy retreat" every three years. The first year, they hammered out new ideas. In year two, they put them into practice. During year three, everyone forgot to track outcomes. By the time year four arrived, they had no data to evaluate if their tactics worked. The next retreat was guesswork all over again. If they had set more consistent mini-assessments (like every 12-15 months), they would have caught the slip earlier and pivoted with less drama.

Remember, the beauty of ImpactOS lies in its flexibility and customization. Your Rhythmic Trigger might be longer or shorter than we suggest. However, the first time you build in a Rhythmic Trigger, it's usually helpful to start with the sweet spot that works well for most nonprofits: *Every 12 months.*

The rhythm needs to be:

1. Short Enough to Stay Relevant

   If you wait too long, the world changes under your feet. Donor communication preferences might shift from Facebook to TikTok, or digital wallets might become the new norm. A shorter assessment and recalibration cycle ensures you don't drift too far behind.

2. Long Enough to Gather Data

   If you pivot tactics every quarter, you never get a solid baseline. Fundraising is cyclical: annual events, year-end campaigns, etc. Wait at least one or two cycles to see genuine results.

Possible Outcomes of a Refresh

When your 12-month refresh window arrives, you will likely land on one of these conclusions:

- **Minor Tweaks:** The fundamentals hum along nicely, but slight adjustments are needed. Consider adding a monthly giving option or refining your event.

- **Moderate Overhaul:** Some tactics are stale, staff capacity might shift, or new technologies beckon. You keep 50–60% of your existing approach while layering in new elements.
- **Major Rethink:** Hitting a wall? Is it under 50% efficiency? You might invest in tactics, cut an old event, or adopt a robust CRM. This demands more time and planning.
- **Call in Reinforcements:** If your results are poor or your staff is overwhelmed, you might need to hire some 1099 bandwidth or, in some circumstances, make tough choices about people's employment. After working with hundreds of nonprofits, we estimate that about 60% of those that have worked on their Refresh realized that the upgrade they needed required an additional investment of funds, generally in training, technology, or additional staff.

Conclusion

Fundraising isn't just about tactics. It's about a coherent system that is fueling your mission. Too many organizations chase shiny events, pray-to-the-almighty-grant-gods, crank out direct mail, or lean on a few heroic donors, only to end up with an exhausted team and unpredictable revenue.

The real breakthrough comes when you align the three essentials: Right-Sized Bandwidth, an Updated Playbook, and Rhythmic Triggers.

When that happens, development shifts from a frantic scramble to a steady, sustainable rhythm. That's how nonprofits move from survival mode to sustainability. Deep conviction about your organization's mission is vital for Development, but the margin for strategic relational infrastructure with your donor base is just as urgent. If your staff is stretched too thin or your tactics are outdated, your conviction alone won't carry you far.

In this era, nonprofits that merge heartfelt relationship-building with data-driven strategy have a colossal edge in the ultra-competitive landscape of nonprofit giving. Why? Because the vast majority of organizations still operate on guesswork or cling to rigid traditions.

Yes, it is extra work to constantly re-evaluate your staff capacity, refresh your fundraising toolbox, and schedule triggers for periodic tune-ups. But the payoff is enormous. Less daily stress, more predictable revenue, and stronger donor loyalty. That kind of stability frees you to focus on your real passion: delivering mission impact!

Remember, the Impact Operating System is about customizing a holistic framework that ensures every component—Vision, Strategy, Culture, Metrics, People, Systems, and Rhythms—syncs together and moves the mission forward in harmony. Development is no different. Get your Sustainable Development Formula right, and you'll watch your mission flourish in ways you never thought possible.

The world needs your mission to succeed, and fresh, sustainable fundraising is what fuels that success for years to come. The leadership team's job is to work the formula so that when asked to give to your mission, people can't wait to say yes.

Most nonprofits haven't cracked this code yet. With the help of the Impact Operating System, you can.

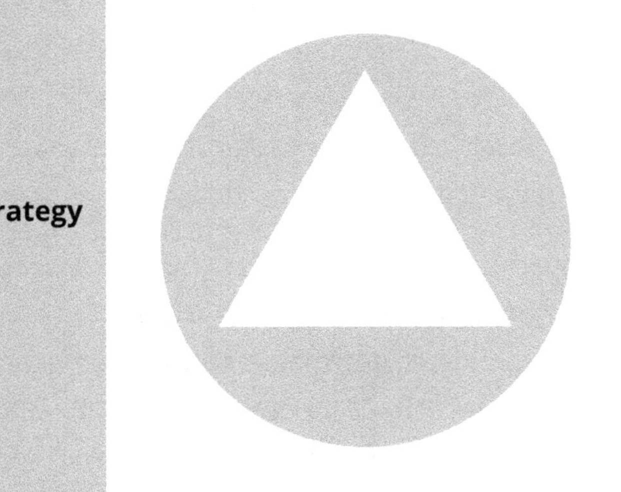

Only 29% of nonprofits accurately measure their impact.

5

METRICS

You want a 360-degree view of what's happening in your nonprofit: missionally, financially, and operationally. You want to know which programs are making a measurable difference, which ones are stuck in neutral, which development efforts are delivering the highest return, and whether your team's efforts are producing meaningful change. While it may seem counterintuitive, metrics are the window.

Metrics support your Vision.

They sharpen your Strategy.

They strengthen Development.

They mold Culture.

They enhance Systems.

They guide People.

And they shape your Rhythms.

Metrics don't have to be relegated to a cold, corporate exercise. They are a tool of Vision and stewardship. They ensure that the resources entrusted to you—time, money, talent—are focused where they matter most. The best organizations use metrics not to assign blame, but to illuminate the path forward. Not to constrain the mission, but to unleash its full potential.

The point is not simply to convince you to use metrics. It's to use meaningful ones.

Why is it, then, that only 29% of nonprofits feel confident they are accurately measuring their impact and effectiveness?

Peter Drucker famously said, "What you measure, you manage." That's the simple idea steering this chapter. To be clear, not everything is easy to quantify, and numbers aren't the only thing that matters in leadership. You might worry that metrics will squeeze the heart out of your mission. Still, used well, metrics can be a strong tool on your belt.

The best organizations use metrics to unleash their mission's full potential.

In this chapter on Metrics, we will explore:

- Why nonprofits struggle with metrics
- Why metrics matter to nonprofits
- The Impact Dashboard Tool and Best Practices

Why Nonprofits Struggle with Metrics

You already know this, but we will say it anyway: Every nonprofit uses metrics. Every organization and every leader is counting something. Maybe it's how many people showed up to the last event, how the budget looks this quarter, or how often donors respond to email.

Not only does every nonprofit use metrics, they also have a scoreboard. The difference is whether it is intentionally aligned with impact, or accidental (or even misleading). Count the wrong things, and it can feel like you're winning when you're actually drifting. Count the right things, and you begin to see clearly what's working and what's not. It empowers your team to make wise, courageous decisions.

The point is not simply to convince you to use metrics. It's to use meaningful ones.

Metrics that map directly to your mission. Metrics that measure progress, not just busyness. If your goal is to change lives, not just survive, you need numbers that tell the truth about your impact, not the story you hope is true.

Still, many nonprofits struggle to get this right. Why? Let's unpack some of the most common challenges:

1. Lack of Clarity on What to Measure:

Many nonprofits know they need metrics but struggle to identify the ones that genuinely reflect their impact. It's tempting to rely on easy-to-track indicators—like newsletter subscribers, event attendance, or social media followers—rather than metrics tied to meaningful change from your "change theory." The result? Data that looks good on paper, but is not able to inform strategy or give any indication of whether you're fulfilling your mission.

2. Resource Constraints and Limited Expertise:

Many nonprofits run lean operations. The staff member tasked with metrics may already be juggling other roles. Without the right tools, training, or dedicated time, tracking metrics can stall before it takes off. And even when data is collected, limited experience with analysis can leave teams unsure how to interpret it. Metrics start to feel like a chore instead of a core function.

3. Fear of What the Numbers Might Say:

Nonprofits worry that lackluster results will scare away donors. That fear can lead to cherry-picking data or avoiding honest evaluation altogether. Ironically, the reluctance to confront hard truths prevents the very progress that honest metrics would inspire. Instead of seeing data as a threat, remember that donors appreciate honesty. When you acknowledge weaknesses and show how you plan to address them, rather than eroding credibility, you earn it.

4. Believing That Data-Driven Decision-Making Kills Passion:

Some organizations value intuition, storytelling, or tradition over analytics. Staff may see metrics as cold or impersonal. We regularly hear the statement, "Numbers don't have heart and kill passion!" Shifting this mindset requires leadership to model curiosity and show that *data is a companion to passion, not a replacement for it.* With time and trust, teams can learn to see data as a trustworthy guide rather than a threat.

5. Overcomplication and Data Overload:

Trying to measure everything is not helpful. Simplicity is your friend. A focused, lightweight metrics framework is far more likely to be used by the staff. So, begin small. Choose what matters most. Let early wins build confidence, then expand from there.

Collecting, analyzing, and contextualizing the right metrics is a lot of work. But the juice is worth the squeeze.

Why Metrics Matter to Nonprofits

Imagine steering a ship through a foggy sea without navigation tools. You might move forward, but you're never quite sure if you're on course. For a nonprofit, metrics act like a compass and a map combined. They reveal where you are, where you are headed, and whether you need to adjust your sails.

Metrics are not about satisfying some external demand. They are about embracing a responsibility to learn and improve. Beth Kanter & Katie Delahaye Paine make the point, "Measurement is not an optional activity. It's the cornerstone of continuous improvement." By collecting meaningful data, you empower your organization to serve your community more effectively.

It's not enough to count heads in the room and call it success. Mario Morino's words from *Leap of Reason* guide us here: "Manage to outcomes, not just to activities." In other words, if your mission is to improve literacy rates, don't just measure how many books you distribute. Track reading comprehension scores, graduation rates, or the number of children who move from struggling to thriving readers.

When metrics reflect your mission, they gain meaning, and your team rallies behind them. When metrics feel disconnected from the mission, they become noise—just another spreadsheet no one reads. Maybe no one really loves the task of submitting numbers that take them out of the flow of everyday work, but when those numbers clearly show how today's work drives tomorrow's change, they become fuel for focus and momentum. In that way, metrics stop being just a report and start becoming a rallying cry.

Done well, metrics transform your nonprofit into a learning organization by informing choices about where to invest your limited resources. This then allows you to quickly adapt to what works and pivot away from what does not. This shift moves metrics from a chore to a gift. It's an invitation to grow, refine, and better serve those who rely on your efforts.

At an existential level, the metrics aren't actually about you or your organization. They're about the change you want to see happen in the world!

Keep in mind that you have to be cautious. Collecting too much data leads to confusion. Mary Kay Gugerty & Dean Karlan remind us to "Collect just enough data to learn and improve." Not too much, not too little. Just the right amount that guides strategic decisions.

At an existential level, the metrics aren't actually about you or your organization. They're about the change you want to see happen in the world.

With all that said, what should you measure? How do you collect it? Once you have the numbers, how do you make sense of what they're telling you? The Impact Dashboard Tool is a helpful framework for answering these questions.

The Impact Dashboard Tool

The Impact Dashboard is a set of metrics (between 9 and 15 key numbers) that capture what matters most to your organization. These are not just data points; they tell the story of your progress toward meaningful outcomes. It's a snapshot of your nonprofit's health and impact at any given moment by bringing clarity to where your leadership team needs to focus next.

Notice the circles in the template below. Each one represents a core metric that you have determined is essential to track. You will replace the generic title "Metric #1", "Metric #2", etc., under each circle with appropriately designated category titles. Here are a few examples of categories: Operations, Staff, Programming, Volunteers, Community Outreach, Fundraising, etc.

They are also separated into Lead Measures and Lag Measures, which we will define in the next section below.

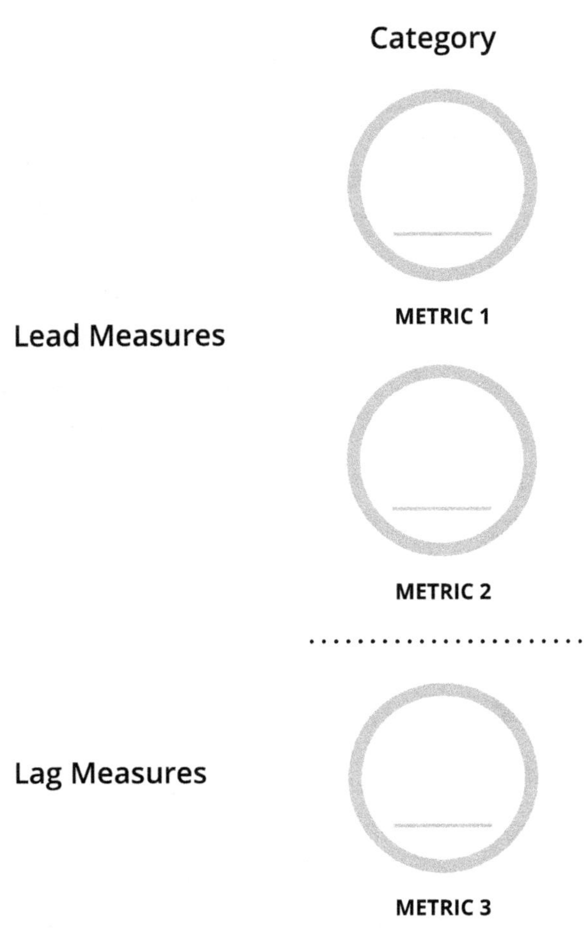

The Impact Dashboard Tool

Three Foundations Upon Which to Build Your Impact Dashboard

Foundation #1: Lead Measures and Lag Measures

When building your dashboard, use a mix of lead and lag measures. Lead measures (Inputs) are the actions or behaviors you track before results show up. They help you see if what you're doing is likely to produce the outcome you want. Lag measures (Outcomes) are the results themselves, which are what you track after the results have already happened.

Lead Measure (Inputs): A lead measure is like checking the oven temperature before baking a cake. If the temperature is correct, the cake will likely turn out well.

Here are some examples:

- **Program Effectiveness:** Number of direct service touchpoints delivered to program participants per week
- **Fundraising:** Number of qualified donor conversations held each month
- **Marketing & Outreach:** Number of new email subscribers added via lead magnets each week
- **Volunteer Engagement:** Number of personalized volunteer check-ins or thank-you texts sent per week
- **Team Health:** Number of weekly team members reporting their top priority and energy level in staff check-ins

Lag Measure (Outcomes): A lag measure is the result you see after the cake is baked—whether it rose nicely or sank in the middle. It's the final proof of success or the sign you need to adjust.

Here are some examples:

- **Program Effectiveness:** Percentage of program participants who achieve their desired outcome or milestone within 90 days of program entry
- **Fundraising:** Total dollars raised from major donors this fiscal year
- **Marketing & Outreach:** Total social media reach across platforms over the last quarter
- **Volunteer Engagement:** Total volunteer hours contributed per month

- **Team Health:** Annual staff turnover rate

By focusing on the right blend, you get real-time feedback (lead measures) to stay on course and proof of success (lag measures) to validate your approach.

Here is the rule of thumb we have for the construction of an Impact Dashboard:

> *For every one Lag Measure you want to see happen, choose two Lead Measures that will drive that outcome.*

This allows you to shift from merely tracking what's already happened (analysis) to actively shaping what comes next (activation). When your metrics are built this way, they don't just report the past; they remind your team that they have the power to change the narrative and make a real impact in their efforts. Metrics then become a tool of agency, not just oversight.

Foundation #2: Include a 360 Degree Picture with Your Metrics

Your Impact Dashboard should feature a mix of Missional, Cultural, and Operational metrics. Why these three things? Because they define what makes a nonprofit truly successful. A nonprofit thrives when its mission is transformative for the people it serves, when its culture is healthy enough that everyone wants to be part of the team and few ever want to leave, and when its operations are sustainable so the organization stays strong, and its finances are both growing and predictable.

Missional Metrics go to the heart of your organization's purpose: What real-world difference are you making in the lives of those you serve or in the broader community? Start with foundational data such as the number of people reached or programs delivered, but don't stop there. Focus on indicators that reflect the quality, depth, and outcomes of your efforts over time. This might include shifts in knowledge, behavior, access, stability, or community conditions. The goal is to measure not just activity, but transformation. This reminds both your team and your stakeholders why your work matters and how it contributes to lasting change. Missional metrics and the long-term change you want to make in the world are why your nonprofit exists in the first place!

Cultural Metrics shine a light on the human side of your organization. These are not about money or outcomes alone; they are about what it feels like to work on your team and partner with your nonprofit. You might survey your staff to gauge job satisfaction, trust in leadership, or alignment with organizational values. Consider adding an annual "culture score" based on factors such as communication quality, sense of purpose, and collaboration across teams. Perhaps you track how many staff and volunteers report feeling confident bringing new ideas forward, or how many beneficiaries feel genuinely heard and respected. Culture metrics can also include staff retention rates, the frequency of team-building activities, or the consistency of peer recognition efforts. Keeping an eye on these numbers ensures that your organization's inner life is healthy.

Operational Metrics help you track the internal engine of your organization—the "nuts and bolts" that keep the machine running. For instance, you might measure monthly revenue or how much you have added to your reserve fund this quarter. You could monitor how closely budget projections match actual spending to ensure you are allocating resources efficiently. Or, you might measure how quickly grant reports are completed, the average volunteer onboarding time, or the percentage of donors who have increased their gift size year-over-year.

Foundation #3: Frequency and Review

In the nonprofit world, metrics lose their power if they're not revisited regularly. That's why your Impact Dashboard can't be static, but should live and breathe alongside your team. Most nonprofits find that weekly, monthly, or quarterly reviews create the right cadence, depending on the metric and the team responsible. Set a rhythm for refreshing and reviewing your Dashboard with intention. Regular updates keep your team focused on what matters. We will address Weekly Impact Check-Ins in Chapter 10: Rhythms, and how they intersect with your metrics review.

Remember: "What you measure, you manage." But it's not solely about managing, it's about adjusting. By reviewing your metrics at consistent intervals, you'll catch trends early, respond with agility, and stay aligned to your Moonshot.

Getting the Impact Dashboard On the Road

To bring the Impact Dashboard to life, we've created a fictional nonprofit, Hope Haven Texas, that resembles a collection of organizations we have worked with. In the example, we mapped out how they might use the Dashboard to track progress, stay focused, and drive meaningful impact. Think of it as a model you can adapt and shape to fit your own organization's mission, context, and goals.

Hope Haven Texas exists to rescue and restore women caught in sex trafficking. They have a clear mission: Remove vulnerable women from dangerous situations into a place of safety, healing, and long-term stability. There's hardly a more noble mission in the world! But how should they measure their success in real time?

At first, they tracked broad, feel-good indicators: number of meals served, Instagram engagement, program attendance, and total social media reach. It all looked impressive in board reports, but the number of women entering their safe houses (their ultimate Missional Lag Measure) was not increasing. The metrics told one story, but the real story was unfolding beneath the surface. Burnover was quietly spreading through the team, volunteers churned faster than they could be trained, and fundraising felt more like a game of chance than a sustainable strategy.

During a staff retreat, the executive director asked a question that was a catalyst for them: *"What if we are counting the wrong things?"*

That set off a journey of trial and error and honest reflection. By incorporating the Impact Dashboard foundations, they began identifying which lead measures influenced the outcomes (what they now call their "life-changing lag measures") they cared about most.

They started experimenting. First, they tracked attendance at weekly outreach events and found that weeks with a higher ratio of volunteers to attendees led to far more inquiries about counseling. That, in turn, correlated directly with more women entering the safe house program—and that metric stuck.

Next, they dug into their development process. Their regular newsletter email blasts weren't moving the needle, but one-on-one sit-downs with donor prospects were. So they added a monthly metric: *number of donor prospect sit-downs*. They did the same for *submitted grants,* tracking how consistently they were hitting grant deadlines. The more they tracked, the more things improved.

At first, they couldn't understand why their volunteers weren't sticking around. They had plenty of interest and signups looked strong, but turnover remained high, and they could see that other volunteers were noticing. After some honest conversations and exit interviews, the problem became clear: volunteers were stepping into emotionally demanding roles without fully understanding what was required, and many felt unprepared, undertrained, or overwhelmed.

So the team redesigned their onboarding process and introduced two new lead measures: the number of expectation-setting conversations

Hope Haven's Impact Dashboard

completed per week, and the number of shadowing hours each volunteer completed before officially starting. These upfront investments slowed down the pipeline but ensured volunteers were mentally and emotionally ready. Over time, retention improved significantly, as evidenced by the lag measure. It wasn't about doing more; it was about doing the proper preparation earlier in the journey.

Internally, the leadership team began holding *quarterly one-on-ones* with staff and implemented a weekly *"must-win" follow-through tracker*. This simple accountability tool kept momentum high without burning people out. *By changing the metric, they changed the outcome.*

Twelve months later, the transformation was measurable: more women in safe houses, healthier staff culture, steady and predictable monthly revenue, and a growing volunteer base.

Finding the right metrics took work. But when they did, every number became a north star.

Impact Dashboard Coaching Tips

1. Be Selective and Strategic

Metrics must fit your organization's capacity and needs. Too many and you're drowning in meaningless data. Too few and you're flying blind. Start small with a few indicators that best capture your essence. Over time, refine these as you learn what is truly helpful. This approach prevents data fatigue and ensures that measurement stays lean, focused, and genuinely beneficial.

2. Metrics Are for Learning, Not Just Reporting

Many leaders initially treat metrics as a box to check for board members or donors. However, we should be ruthless about what we track and whether it helps us make decisions. Use data to discover what works, what doesn't, and how to get better. When something is not yielding results, data points the way forward, allowing you to adjust your approach rather than doubling down on ineffective strategies.

We have used this humorous anecdote a few times when working with nonprofits: A small arts nonprofit once bragged about its monthly newsletter subscriber count by reporting, "We're reaching 10,000 people a month!" The board meetings were filled with excited talk about subscriber growth. But guess what happened when they checked click-through rates and follow-up engagement? Almost no one was reading those newsletters. Engagement was abysmal. Initially, it was an awkward moment, yet it was also liberating. They stopped celebrating vanity metrics and started focusing on meaningful engagement measures. Before long, they tweaked their content, improved open rates, and saw real donor interest rise.

This shift was possible only when they embraced data as a learning tool.

3. Use Metrics to Build Relationships with Donors

Today's donors want assurance that their money leads to real change. Instead of resenting this scrutiny, treat it as an opportunity to build trust. Show donors what you measure, why you measure it, and what you have learned, even if some findings are less than perfect. Honest, data-backed narratives foster credibility that leads to increased funding.

4. Find the Digital Platform That's Right for Your Organization

Technology plays a role, too. Tools and platforms increase accessibility and simplify data collection, storage, and analysis. If you have the right platform, it can be easy and efficient to track your most important metrics, uncover patterns, identify what resonates, and pinpoint where energy is wasted.

That's why we created the ImpactHub app. It's a digital platform that houses your entire ImpactOS, including your key metrics, in one place. It's built to make leading, managing, and executing easier and more practical.

Whatever you choose for your platform, remember to keep it simple. Overloading your team with complex dashboards and analytics formulas can backfire. Start with what is practical and scale up as you gain comfort and proficiency.

5. Use Metrics to Support Your Strategic Planning

Every monthly review meeting should revisit your goals and check if your chosen metrics show progress. If the data suggests stagnation, don't panic. Instead, celebrate that you caught the problem early and can pivot. Without metrics, you're left guessing, possibly repeating ineffective approaches *for years.*

Conclusion

Trying to lead a nonprofit without meaningful metrics is like searching for a black cat in a locked basement at night with all the lights off. They are not about nitpicking or judging your efforts. They are about shining a light on the path forward, helping ensure you are truly fulfilling your mission.

Yes, metrics can feel intimidating. Yes, you might discover outcomes that fall short of your aspirations. But that's the point: growth and learning are at the heart of this work. By embracing metrics, you give yourself and your team the chance to refine your approach, deepen your impact, and maintain the trust of donors and communities.

When everyone understands what is being measured and why, the entire organization gains momentum. The rotary engine of your Impact Operating System moves forward with purpose and energy.

Metrics matter. Let's make them matter for the right reasons.

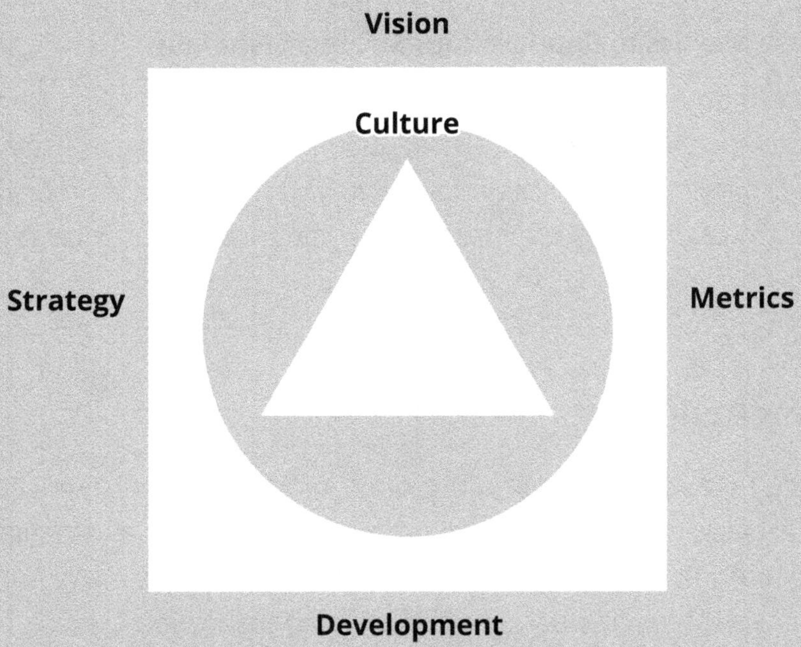

Vision

Culture

Strategy

Metrics

Development

Nonprofits with intentional, healthy cultures see a 43% increase in productivity.

6

CULTURE

According to national statistics, over 2.5 million seniors in the U.S. are homebound. Most of those seniors live alone. We had the privilege of working with one nonprofit that served this often overlooked group of people. The team was out on the road most days, going from house to house giving of themselves to each elderly person by offering them the dignity they deserved.

The team's hearts were full, the calendar was packed, and the work was heavy. The classic symptoms began to surface: rushed handoffs, unclear ownership, and broken communication. It wasn't a program problem. It was a culture problem.

Culture is the multiplier that helps your team thrive and your mission endure.

Seeing this, the Executive Director made a bold decision: create an intentional culture that is healthy rather than settling for a reactive culture that was unhealthy.

They started small. Every staff meeting began with a "mission moment," celebrating one story of impact. They built shared agreements around conflict, decision-making, and staff health. They clarified role expectations, started monthly team check-ins, and launched a simple peer recognition ritual called "The Impact Shoutout."

Things slowly began to change, and momentum built. Within six months, team communication significantly improved and morale lifted. Collaboration increased, and deadlines were met without burnout. Staff began proactively fixing systems instead of reacting to problems.

Within a year and a half, their team testified to the significant organizational about-face as they almost doubled their impact. They didn't add new staff or land a flashy new grant. They simply invested precious energy into their culture-making, and it changed the game.

Their Executive Director told us, "We used to survive on passion alone, but it wasn't enough. When we started treating culture like something we could create and shape, things started to change. It didn't happen overnight. But I actively watched as the energy in our team increased every week. We're not just surviving the work anymore. We're energized by it."

Here's what we know:

> *Nonprofits that invest in intentional cultural practices see a 43% increase in productivity within 18 months.*

Isn't that crazy?! Culture is the multiplier that helps your team thrive and your mission endure.

Most of us would admit that organizational culture is essential, but when your to-do list stretches a mile long and you are functioning on a shoestring budget, spending the energy and effort to build a strong, intentional culture often slips to the bottom of the list.

And that's precisely why so many nonprofit teams stall out – not for lack of passion, but for lack of clarity, rhythm, and shared expectations. People show up because they believe in the mission. But they stay, or leave, because of the culture.

People show up because they believe in the mission. But they stay or leave because of the culture.

So, how do you build a team culture that leads to missional impact, where everyone wants to stay and no one wants to leave?

In this chapter, we will explore the following big topics:

- Four Kinds of Nonprofit Culture
- How Values Shape Your Culture
- The Culture Making Tool

Four Kinds of Nonprofit Culture

Nonprofit leadership differs starkly from business life. You're corralling a diverse team—some full-time, some part-time, many volunteers—while navigating a labyrinth of board opinions, donor expectations, and community needs. The stakes are mission-critical: real lives, real communities.

Simon Sinek highlights in *Leaders Eat Last*, "A nonprofit's mission can't flourish if the team feels expendable." What makes the team feel expendable? They are underpaid, overstretched, and left to scrape by with minimal training. They're showing up with passion, but few are set up to thrive. In fact, it's common for nonprofit employees to take a "passion pay cut" of 30–50% compared to their private-sector peers. They accept it because they believe in the cause.

That conviction is beautiful, but it is both a blessing and a curse: you get team members with huge hearts, but sometimes misaligned roles, mismatched skills, or minimal support. Over time, the cracks of fatigue, churn, and lost momentum begin to show.

That is why the first lever to pull is culture, not more effort. Culture is "how we do things around here." It is the shared values, norms, and rhythms that turn big hearts into consistent outcomes. When you invest in culture, you give people clear roles, healthy expectations, and simple habits that protect passion from burnout. You build trust and create momentum that does not depend on heroics. In short, culture is the multiplier that helps your team thrive and your mission endure.

To make this practical, let's name what culture looks like in real life. In our work, four common patterns show up again and again. Treat them as a mirror, not a verdict. Identify where you are today, then use the tools that follow to move toward a healthier, higher-impact culture.

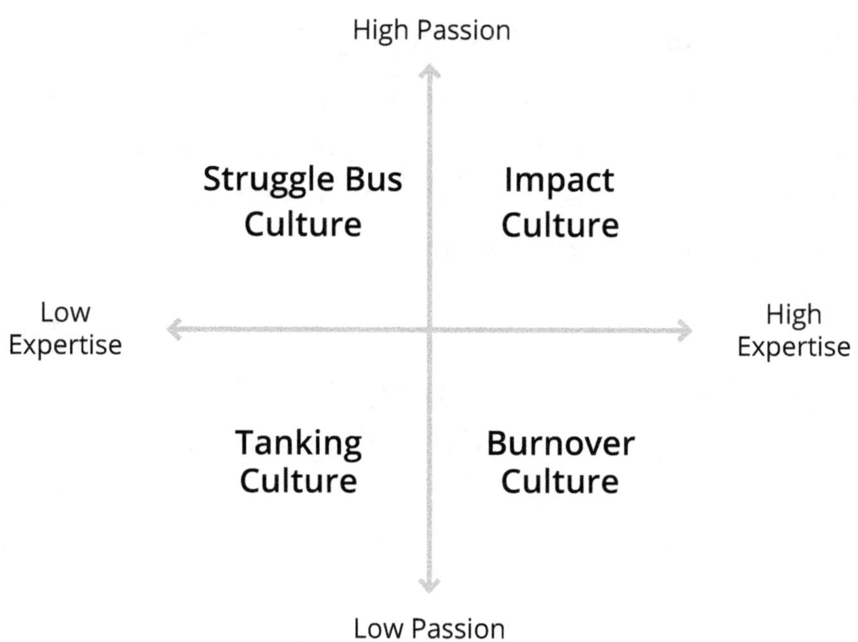

1. Struggle Bus Culture: High Passion / Low Expertise

The staff is deeply passionate. They would do just about anything for the mission. But they may lack specialized skills or similar work experience. Generally speaking, their day-to-day impact is blunted because they may lack the skills to deliver on the role they find themselves in.

2. Tanking Culture: Low Passion / Low Expertise

Typically, this is a nonprofit that has lost its spark. The staff is on autopilot. They are not incompetent *per se*, but they don't invest in upskilling or fresh ideas, and they lack a passionate connection to the mission. Apathy, cynicism, clock punchers, and stagnant programs abound.

3. Burnover Culture: Low Passion / High Expertise

Here you will find skilled staff who may have come from corporate backgrounds but now have little emotional investment in the nonprofit anymore. They are bored or frustrated, and as a result, the mission feels more like a job than a calling. This is the fastest route to high turnover.

4. Impact Culture: High Passion / High Expertise

This is the sweet spot. The team is passionate, well-equipped, and skilled. They constantly refine their skills, hold each other accountable, and see how their sacrifice fuels genuine mission progress. In this environment, staff retention is high, and volunteers sense a strong, purposeful energy.

Culture is the oil that keeps your nonprofit engine running smoothly. Without it, friction builds.

Take a moment and chart where your organization currently stands in this matrix. Be ruggedly honest. If you're bold, ask three of your teammates to do the same. You have nothing to lose.

Regardless of where you currently stand on this matrix, everyone wants a culture marked by both High Passion and High Expertise. After all, that's likely why you are reading this book. So, how do you craft a team culture that nurtures both the heart and the professional competency needed to deliver real impact?

Culture Making: The Skill Set of the Future

The existence of culture in every organization is an inevitability. The question is this: Will you intentionally build a healthy culture, or will you be accidental and allow it to happen to you? Culture is the oil that keeps your nonprofit engine running smoothly. Without it, friction builds. The good news is that intentional culture building is a skill set that can be learned, refined, and practiced.

You can have the most brilliant strategic plan in the world, but as our friend Patrick Lencioni reminds us, "A splintered group can derail even the best strategies." It's been said that "Culture eats strategy for breakfast." This rings especially true in nonprofits, where short resources and big passion collide.

How Values Shape Your Culture

In every nonprofit, values shape the way people lead, relate, and make decisions. To build a thriving culture, it helps to distinguish between three distinct types of organizational values: Aspirational Values, External Values, and Internal Work Values. But here's what you need to know: not all values are created equal or have the same amount of culture-shaping power.

Aspirational Values name who you are becoming, not who you are today. They emerge when your team identifies a gap between your current reality and your desired future. Maybe you list "equity" as a core value, even though your leadership team, hiring practices, or community partnerships don't yet fully reflect it. That's not disingenuous—it's directional.

But here's the caution: if more than half of your stated values describe a version of your culture that does not yet exist, people notice. It can lead to disillusionment, cynicism, and disengagement. Instead of uniting your team, your values become a mirror reflecting the gap between what's said and what's lived.

External Values are the values you choose to communicate to your donors, volunteers, influencers, and community. They are part of your public identity that you want the world to associate with your mission. These often show up in taglines, websites, or fundraising appeals. For example, a youth-serving nonprofit might highlight values like "empowerment," "dignity," or "access." These values help you connect with your external stakeholders and establish credibility.

Internal Work Values, meanwhile, are the most operationally important—and the most overlooked and underutilized. These define how your team chooses to work together: how you make decisions, give feedback, resolve tension, or celebrate wins. Think of values like "Humble Service," "Trusting Relationships," or "Disciplined Innovation." These are not branding tools or wishful thinking. They are the day-to-day social contracts that shape how your team functions.

Each type of value plays a role. But clarity matters. Confusing them or treating all values the same can lead to misalignment and culture drift. When leaders clearly name each type, they foster trust, reduce friction, and build a thriving culture.

The Impact Operating System is designed to build internal alignment, so we will exclusively focus on Internal Work Values. Unlike external or aspirational values, internal values are immediately actionable. They define how people treat each other, make decisions, and collaborate day to day. If culture is "Whatever is normal for a group of people," then internal values are the blueprint. By anchoring the system in these behaviors, the ImpactOS helps teams build consistency, alignment, and momentum from the inside out.

Your Values tell your team what you want to be normal.

These Values act as the internal compass for your nonprofit's teamwork culture. They are not just lofty ideals posted on a wall or in an annual report. For example, if one of your desired norms is *Joyful Collaboration*, that's far more specific than *Teamwork*. *Joyful Collaboration* implies a shared belief that collaboration should be infused with optimism and a genuine sense of connection that goes beyond mere cooperative tasks. These values speak directly to how you want your staff to behave within the organization, *rather than describing how you want to appear to the public.*

On our team, we use five values:

- **Humble Posture:** Putting others first, deferring glory, serving others first in a generous way.
- **Trusting Relationships:** Contending for the highest possible good through calibrating support and challenge.
- **Co-creative Collaboration:** Shared influence that leverages each other's strengths in the creative and delivery process.
- **Self-directed Initiative:** Supporting each other by executing agreed-upon outcomes and communicating promptly.
- **Disciplined Process:** Trusting and acting upon deliberately created plans with efficiency and follow-through.

These values serve as daily guardrails for how we want to function and what we want to be "normal." A guardrail is a protective boundary that keeps things from veering dangerously off course. It doesn't restrict movement, but it does prevent a drift into dysfunction. In the context of culture, values offer a shared standard for how people make decisions and relate to one another, especially under pressure. They create clarity around what "normal" looks like – so teams can move faster, with more trust and less friction.

Chances are, our values listed above mean very little to you. And that's the point. Those values represent *our* mission and *our* team. They speak a world of insight into our culture.

What should they be for your culture and team?

Now that you have a sense of what internal, team-oriented values are, the next question is: How do you translate those values into practical realities? Values are only as good as they make their way into embodied practices of those values! If they don't, it's just words on a piece of paper.

The Culture Making Tool will help you bring them to life by showing how they converge to shape a culture that attracts great people and gives them a reason to stay.

The Culture Making Tool

Sociologists propose nine essential elements that build culture, but that's a lot for even the very best leaders to keep straight, much less integrate into their organization! So we will focus on four because we believe they yield maximum payoff for nonprofits.

P – Practices

L – Language

A – Artifacts

N – Narratives

Each of these four elements (P.ractices, L.anguage, A.rtifacts, and N.arratives) are how the values you have selected come to life as your team experiences, expresses, and reinforces them every day. Think of P.L.A.N. as the blueprint for embedding culture into the rhythms of your organization.

While we double-click on each of these elements, we will illustrate them by using the example of Alcoholics Anonymous (AA). While not a classic nonprofit, it's a social movement with arguably one of the most transformative, culture-rich approaches in modern history. We will then give you an action step to take, some hard-earned coaching insights, and pitfalls to avoid.

P - Practices Embed Culture

Practices are the regular activities and habits that embed culture into the daily life of an organization. In AA, the core practices revolve around the 12 Steps. These steps are not just a pamphlet; they are a guide that members actively follow, reinforcing accountability, mutual support, and personal growth. By having everyone commit to these practices, AA ensures that the culture's values of honesty, humility, and perseverance are continually reaffirmed.

In your nonprofit, practices might include weekly check-ins where everyone shares a quick "win" from their work, or a monthly "mission moment" where a beneficiary's story is read aloud. The key is to align practices with your chosen values so that the team's daily behaviors embody those values. If one of your values is *Radical Candor* a practice could be a 5-minute debrief of every meeting where you evaluate how the meeting could improve (You can do a quick debrief using these three questions each time: What worked? What didn't work? What do we need to do differently?).

Your values are only as good as the practices everyone uses to embody them.

Action Step: Create one practice for each core value that embeds your culture in every person and team.

Coaching Tips:

1. Tie the Practices to the Value:

   If you value *Generous Collaboration*, a practice might be "Every project has a cross-department co-lead to encourage working across teams."

2. Keep the Practice Simple:

   If you value *Disciplined Process*, a practice might be "We respond to internal emails within 24 hours."

3. Designate a Champion:

   For each practice, designate a team member responsible for ensuring it occurs.

Pitfall: Don't try to change everything at once. If your staff is used to chaotic 2-hour meetings, shifting to 15-minute daily huddles can spark resentment if done without explanation or training. Communicate the "why" and demonstrate how a new practice genuinely benefits staff.

One of the organizations we worked with that has a very unique mission, tried a daily team "silence practice" for 45 minutes at 9 a.m. The idea? Encourage reflection. The result? People kept forgetting to be silent, and most of the team found it awkward. They adjusted it to "silent half-Mondays," once a week, accompanied by gentle background music, and found a sweet spot. Culture is iterative. Some initial ideas might flop, and that's okay.

L - Language Creates Culture

Abraham Joshua Heschel once said, "Words create worlds." He was right—language shapes the way we see, feel, and behave. In any organization, language becomes the scaffolding of culture. Specific phrases or responses evolve into shorthand for a team's identity and shared values.

Consider AA, where phrases like "Thank you for sharing," "Keep coming back," or "If you work it, it works" consistently reinforce a culture of support, accountability, and progress, without judgment.

For your team, language might look like a meaningful phrase attached to each value. If *Joyful Collaboration* is one of your values, the phrase might be: "Team up. Light up." Over time, when a challenging project hits, someone might say it with a grin – half playful, entirely intentional. That simple cue reinforces what your culture is meant to be.

Culture is often more caught than taught. Language is how people catch it.

Action Step: Introduce meaningful, memorable, and inspirational catchphrases—one per value—that will create and reinforce your culture in everyday moments.

Coaching Tips:

1. Make Them Memorable:

   The well-known Chick-fil-A value of Hospitality is embodied by employees who are trained to say, "My pleasure." In fact, it is so memorable that an urban legend has surfaced that if an employee fails to say the phrase, you get your meal free.

2. Make Them Meaningful:

   If your value is *Mutual Accountability*, staff might say "Remember, it's a two-way street" when discussing deadlines or feedback loops. This emphasizes the need for reciprocity among the team.

3. Make Them Inspirational:

   For a value like *Bold Consistency*, staff may end a meeting by saying together the phrase, "Stand Steady. Step Forward!"

Pitfall: Overly forced language feels unnatural; staff won't adopt it. Let the team co-create a phrase they find fun or practical. When co-ownership occurs, the language "sticks" far better. A small environmental nonprofit tried a pun-laden lexicon, like "sun-ergy" (for synergy). But staff found it cringeworthy. Eventually, they landed on a single phrase: "Green checks," meaning "We check everything we do for eco-friendliness." That one soared. Everyone joked, "Did this pass the green check test?" It wasn't just catchy. It became a guiding cue that kept their daily work aligned with the organization's purpose.

A - Artifacts Embody Culture

Artifacts are tangible objects or physical symbols that reinforce cultural meaning. Humans are embodied beings who have always used artifacts like wedding rings, plaques, and merit badges to mark identity and commitment to a particular tribe, mission, or milestone. An artifact is something you give someone that engages one or more of the five senses. Something they can see, hear, touch, taste, or smell.

In AA, participants earn chips for sobriety milestones. They treasure it and carry it around with them, often in their pocket, because of its significance. And when they feel the urge to take a drink, they hold their chip and remember how important it is to them. A simple coin becomes a powerful token that whispers, "You've come this far; keep going!"

In a nonprofit, artifacts can be similarly meaningful. Instead of a million items of random swag (t-shirts, YETI mugs, Moleskine books, koozies, and keychains galore), consider giving new team members a small object that symbolizes your mission.

We have worked with the executive team of the Department of Education in a particular state. After helping them create their internal work values, they delegated the responsibility of creating an artifact to represent their six values. One individual who does woodworking as a hobby identified six different types of wood—one representing each value—and beautifully crafted a block with each type connected to the others. He explained the symbolism in a short video that the team watched together. It wasn't just symbolic; it became a shared, tactile cue that anchored their values in something real. Every time they turned the block to highlight a different piece of wood, it reminded them who they were and how they aspired to lead.

Artifacts don't just decorate our environments; they shape them. And as we'll explore more deeply in Chapter 7: People, helping your team find and attach meaning to their work isn't just a nice bonus. It's a critical lever for engagement, retention, belonging, and long-term impact.

Artifacts should be authentic and thoughtful, not just another cheap knick-knack collecting dust.

Action Step: Create an artifact that solidifies your culture.

Coaching Tips: There are three types of artifacts. We recommend you choose one to begin with and add the others as you go.

1. Mantra Artifacts:
    i. Definition: A mantra is a short, memorable phrase or statement that expresses a guiding value that inspires. A Mantra Artifact symbolizes the internal work values you have chosen. While it may be challenging to create one that represents them all, there are endless ways to make this artifact, and you can improve as you go.

    ii. Example: A brass cube with an icon of a value on each side.

2. Milestone Artifacts:

    i. Definition: These mark significant accomplishments in someone's role—a moment of "You did it!" These artifacts celebrate progress and connect the achievement to your mission.

    ii. Example: A "1,000 hours volunteered" pin.

3. Marker Artifacts:

    i. Definition: These honor the passage of time and the endurance it represents. They celebrate someone's presence over seasons, not just what they've done, but who they've been.

    ii. Example: On a team member's 5th anniversary, give them a remnant from your original program site. Engrave the word "Steadfast" and give them an accompanying note that says, "This played an important role in our history, just like you. A reminder that the foundation we're building today stands stronger because of your faithful dedication."

Pitfall: Sometimes experiments flop, and that's part of the process. So don't be slow to pivot. One nonprofit handed out "Golden Bean Bag Chairs" to staff who survived an insane year of events. The gesture got laughs at first, but the chairs quickly became hallway clutter. The novelty wore off, so they swapped it for a monthly rotating "Golden Mug" that staff used daily. Turns out, a little practicality goes a long way when it comes to meaningful recognition. Overdoing it with t-shirts, water bottles, or silly trinkets can cheapen the significance of the artifacts with your team.

Here's the Rule of Thumb: *If you've seen it done in a bunch of other places, it's not unique enough for you.*

N - Narratives Spread Culture

Stories shape how people think, feel, and act. Daniel Coyle notes in *The Culture Code*, "Stories carry the DNA of your culture." In nonprofit life, storytelling is already central. Stories are used to inspire donors, mobilize volunteers, and showcase mission impact. And rightly so. But often, the most powerful stories for shaping culture are the ones told internally.

AA meetings are built around storytelling: real, raw accounts of struggle, growth, failure, and hope. These narratives reinforce shared values, build empathy, and spark belief in transformation.

In your nonprofit, you likely tell donors stories of mission breakthroughs. But what about internal stories that highlight your team's values? If *Resilient Hope* is one of your values, tell the story of a program coordinator who showed up week after week to an after-school program, even when attendance was spotty and supplies were short. Share how a student pulled her aside and said, "I come here because I know you'll be here." That moment can become more than encouragement; it becomes a story the team tells often, reminding everyone that steady presence in hard places can change lives.

Ultimately, these aren't just stories. They're culture-carriers. Narrative is the most powerful agent that spreads culture. Tell stories often. Let them become your organizational folklore, passed down, retold, and lived out.

Action Step: Identify and share stories that spread your cultural values. If you're using the ImpactHub app, capture Values and Impact Stories there so you don't forget them!"

Coaching Tips: There are two types of narratives to tell.

1. Origin Story Narrative: This is the origin tale of how your nonprofit

started or discovered its niche more deeply. The Executive Director of one of the organizations we worked with that serves people with an addiction and people experiencing homelessness went undercover with his son in the homeless community to experience firsthand a taste of what life was like. The lessons they learned were so influential on them that they helped shape the organization into what it is today. That story was a cornerstone for onboarding new staff and volunteers, and raising money from donors.

2. Cultural Hero Narratives: These are anecdotes about staff members or volunteers who exemplified the heart of your mission and lived out the cultural values. These stories are told during rhythmic meetings to inspire others and in the onboarding process to communicate the heart of the mission.

Pitfall: Telling the same stale stories year after year without context is a sign that the culture is stuck in the past. Fresh details or newly discovered angles of cornerstone stories keep the narrative power alive. Also, constant farming of new stories from the staff and volunteers will win the day. Beware of exaggerating stories so they become superhuman, as this can damage your credibility.

Conclusion

A state-run Department of Education initially asked for our help with creating a strategic plan. This was a massive undertaking, considering there are more than 750,000 K-12 students and that they manage a $13 billion budget. While technically a government agency, there is significant overlap with nonprofits, as they are mission-driven, externally funded (rather than revenue-based), and subject to board oversight.

After helping them build a strategic plan, they saw a significant jump in the right direction. They are hard chargers attempting to address the tsunami of educational opportunities. The stress and pressure began to show cracks in their team. We reminded them that you can have a compelling Vision, a winning strategy, and all the money in the world, but without a great culture, you won't consistently do great things.

You can have a compelling vision, a winning strategy, and all the money in the world, but without a great culture, you won't do great things consistently.

So, they made a difficult but crucial decision: take the time to purposefully build a healthy culture rather than leaving it to chance. They created clear values and incorporated P.ractices, L.anguage, A.rtifacts, and N.arrative into their agency. Slowly but surely, all the ships in the harbor began to rise as the culture improved. The change was so evident that one national educational consultant said, "What this agency is doing is so innovative that there are only a couple of other states I can think of who would even come close to attempting what they are doing!"

In truth, what they are attempting isn't groundbreaking. It is simply doing the hard work of purposeful culture building that transforms their deeply held sense of calling to impact "every child" from a pipe dream into reality.

In the nonprofit world, it's a tragedy to waste passion in toxic or chaotic environments. If your team is giving you their hearts and showing up, they deserve a culture that lifts them, not drains them: one that helps them love their work, not just the cause.

So let's get to it!

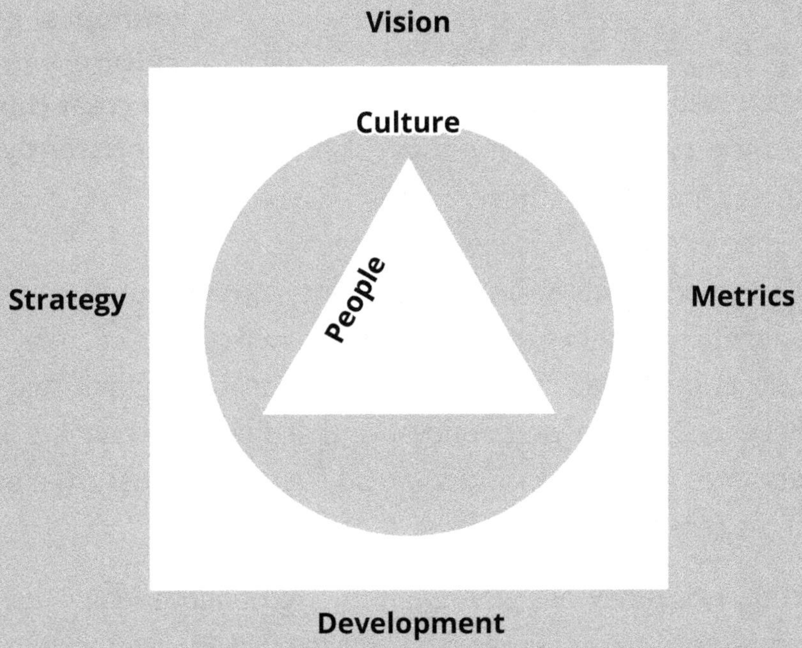

Vision

Culture

People

Strategy

Metrics

Development

93% of nonprofit staff don't understand how their work connects to the organization's strategy.

7

PEOPLE PART 1

Your greatest asset is not a five-year strategic plan or its sleek new facility. It's your people.

Staff, board members, volunteers, and donors play a distinct role in an intricate dance. Peter Drucker said it this way, *"People, not strategies, deliver real results."* Without the right people in the right roles with strong leadership and support, progress stalls. Impact fades. Morale dips. Culture suffers.

The data backs this up:

> *93% of nonprofit employees don't understand how their day-to-day work connects to the organization's larger strategy. And 82% of volunteers and staff report feeling undervalued.*

These aren't just statistics. They're warning lights. Left unaddressed, they slowly drain your mission's momentum.

That's why the following two chapters focus on people.

- Part One (Chapter 7) focuses on the team members: staff, leadership, and board.
- Part Two (Chapter 8) will unpack how the team functions: structures, systems, and alignment.

In this chapter, we will explore what it looks like to assess, support, and unleash the potential of your people. When people are placed well, supported wisely, and deeply connected to the mission, they don't just contribute—they thrive!

We will introduce two tools in this chapter:

- The Right Fit Tool helps assess and develop team members
- The Board Tune-Up Tool helps your board operate at its highest potential

We will also highlight crucial "people practices" to help you sidestep major pitfalls and ensure the humans in your nonprofit are truly your greatest asset and not your biggest hurdle.

The people domain is complex because people are endlessly complex. The tools we are introducing to you are not *simplistic*; they have traveled through *complexity* to arrive at being *simple* and *accessible*.

The Compensation Formula

In the for-profit sector, compensation often boils down to one central question: "What is my salary and benefits package?" Sure, culture matters, but the paycheck tends to loom large. In nonprofits, though, we see something different: people accept lower salaries in exchange for a sense of meaning and passion. This shift is not just a quirk; it's often baked into how nonprofits recruit, retain, and motivate staff.

So let's redefine compensation for nonprofit employees as follows:

Compensation = Money (what they're paid) + Meaning (why they do it).

When a nonprofit job offers a clear sense of *meaning*, it can offset a lower salary. It's often the unspoken social contract. In behavioral economics, this is called a "tradeoff." This intangible piece of *meaning* is a critical part of the deal between nonprofits and their employees.

When you shift organizational priorities, revamp programs, or pivot strategy, you can unintentionally change the meaning side of the equation. Suddenly, the staff member who joined because they believed in hands-on youth mentoring finds themselves stuck behind a desk doing data entry or focusing on a new program that doesn't resonate with them. In effect, their overall compensation (money + meaning) just took a hit, even if their paycheck stayed the same.

Compensation = Money + Meaning.

And because their monetary compensation is already lower than what they might earn elsewhere, frustration can spike quickly.

That's when staff members start wondering, "Am I getting paid enough to do this?" When clarity fades or structures shift without support, even your most committed team members can begin to drift.

One of the nonprofits we worked with, embedded in a neighborhood marked by deep poverty and high rates of violence, has a bold but simple mission: walk with kids from 3rd grade through graduation. In the early days, their approach was deeply relational, organic, unpolished, and run out of the homes of long-term neighborhood residents. It attracted people like Rajon: warm, selfless, magnetic. He was the heartbeat of the place and walked into his role when they were serving fewer than 50 kids *each week.*

But as the organization grew to serving hundreds and hundreds of kids *each day*, so did the complexity. They needed more structure: centralized programming, clearer systems, and consistent oversight. While these changes *looked* less relational on the surface, they were meant to better serve relationships but on a larger scale.

What followed was an 18-month tug-of-war between Rajon and the Executive Team. He wasn't against the mission. But the shift in how the mission was carried out left him disoriented. The version of the nonprofit he had helped build no longer fit him, or he no longer fit it. Once joyful and generous, Rajon became visibly frustrated, hard to engage, and increasingly vocal about his pay. The deeper issue was not about money. It was about *fit*. And in many nonprofits, that quiet drift can turn your brightest lights into your most significant tension points.

To manage this dynamic effectively, nonprofits must be transparent about changes to their vision, strategy, or tactics. If you're going to pivot, involve staff in the conversation. Show them how the shift aligns with your mission. Reaffirm the organization's commitment to core principles. By doing so, you safeguard the meaning component of the Compensation Formula. At times, you might also need to adjust actual salary or benefits to keep pace with market realities or to recognize the extra burden staff are carrying. If you don't, your staff will begin scouring LinkedIn for roles that better meet their financial and meaning needs.

Light Bulb Moment: If you miss the unspoken assumption many nonprofit staff hold, that "meaning makes up part of my paycheck," you risk losing them when strategy shifts, rebrands happen, or operational changes roll out. In other words, when the mission or its delivery changes, it can feel to staff as if they've lost part of their compensation. That emotional and psychological hit is real. And this single blind spot has triggered more staff departures than most budget cuts ever could.

While compensation is not everything, it does serve as a starting point for recognizing that, when it comes to staff, we have to think about "fit" differently.

How (and Why) "Fit" Matters for Nonprofits

You've probably heard Jim Collins's famous metaphor about "getting the right people on the bus." In a nonprofit, not only do you need them on the bus, you also need them in the correct seats, heading to the right destination, at a ticket price they can afford.

People are often in nonprofits because of deep-seated values and personal convictions. If they are not aligned with the culture, the role, and the organization's financial and emotional realities, they will leave, or worse, *stay and disengage.*

We once heard of this conversation from a management class at Harvard University, and it stuck with us. The professor put up a version of the following picture on a screen:

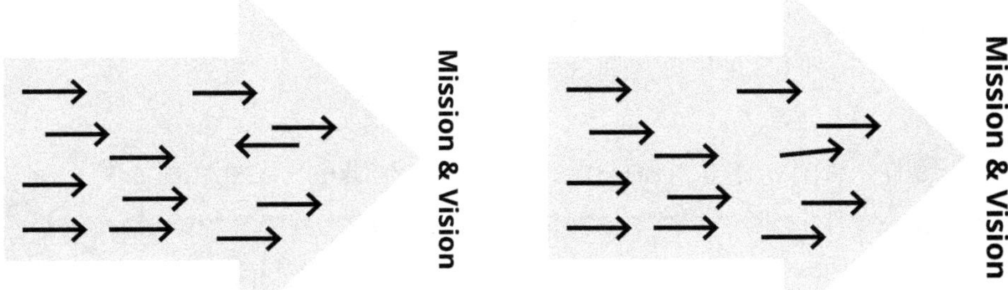

He then asked the class, "Which picture demonstrates the most danger for an organization?" As you might expect, almost all of the class said it was the big arrow on the left, because one of the smaller arrows inside it was pointed in the complete opposite direction.

"It's the big arrow on the right," he said. "That little arrow inside it may only be a few degrees off, but it has enough power to lead a lot of the other arrows in that direction, too. And the next thing you know? The whole organization is in a different place than they wanted to be."

This illustration ultimately boils down to *fit*. Nonprofit culture isn't monolithic. Some are agile and entrepreneurial, others steady and tradition-bound. For staff, you can't just check a skills box on a resumé; you have to ensure the candidate's style, motivations, and expectations sync with your organization's core values.

Consider this: a marketing expert might be stellar at campaign design but could become restless if your culture is slow and deliberative. They're not a good fit. Alternatively, a deeply caring social worker might struggle at a data-driven organization where every outcome is charted and measured. Worse still, if people feel either money or meaning does not adequately compensate them, they will question their role daily: "Is this worth it?"

That's where our central question emerges: *How do you know if someone fits your organization, and how can you develop them toward that fit over time?*

People Tool #1: The Right Fit Tool

We have always appreciated the People Analyzer Tool from the book *Traction* as an innovative, simple, practical tool for businesses. But nonprofits are a different world. The dynamics of compensation, culture, and motivation are far more nuanced. You are often working with passionate people who have taken a "calling over paycheck" approach, and that changes everything. So while the People Analyzer offers a solid foundation, it does not fully account for the unique realities of nonprofit leadership. That is why we have adapted a few core principles, reimagined, and recontextualized them through the lens of nonprofit life. The Right Fit Tool honors the previously mentioned complexities while still helping leaders assess, support, and develop their teams with clarity.

The Right Fit Tool is designed to help answer the question: "Is this person a good fit in our nonprofit?" It also helps you and your team assess (and then develop) each staff member or prospective hire according to three essential criteria:

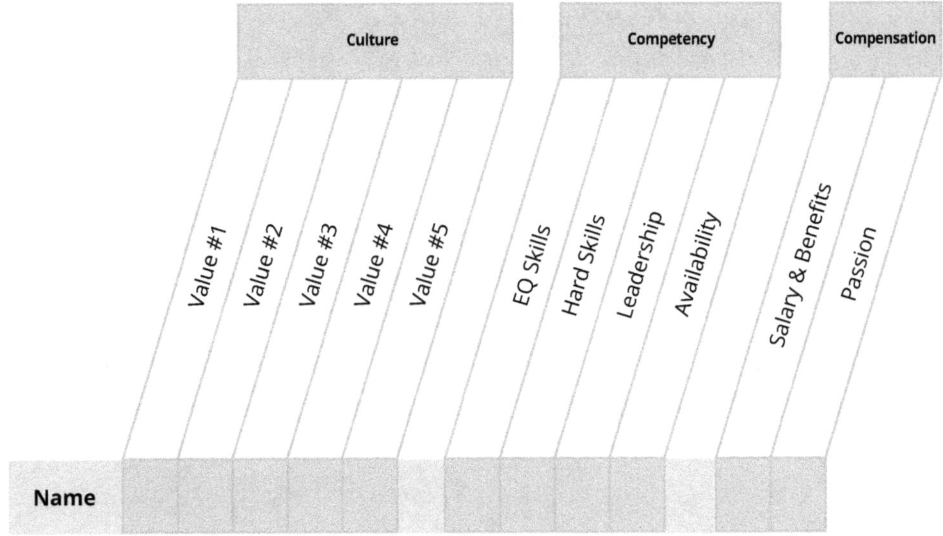

1. **Culture Fit: Is everyone playing the same song?**

   Having the right people in the right seats isn't just about skills; it's about alignment with your values. Culture Fit helps you assess whether team members thrive in your organization's unique rhythm and embody the behaviors that define your identity. It's not about forced uniformity, but shared conviction. Use the questions below to spark honest reflection in one-on-ones and team conversations.

   Evaluative Questions:

   i. Do they share our core values?

   ii. Do they thrive in the pace, dynamic, and ethos of our nonprofit?

   Example: One of the organizations we worked with developed the following evaluative questions from each of their five Internal Work Values. They used these questions with their staff to spark conversation in their one-on-ones.

i. **Trusting Relationships:** How consistently do you assume the best in others, even when mistakes are made?

ii. **Authentic Empowerment:** How consistently do you give team members the space, support, and authority to solve problems without stepping in?

iii. **Humble Service:** How consistently do you offer your time and talents generously, without seeking recognition or status?

iv. **Generous Collaboration:** How consistently do you actively seek input from others and also lend help to co-create on projects?

v. **Disciplined Innovation:** How consistently do you champion or put forward ideas, even when success is not ensured?

Culture fit is your rhythm section. The drummer and bass lock the tempo, so everything else holds together. If your bassist is playing indie rock when your nonprofit needs bluegrass, you get chaos instead of harmony. Culture fit ensures everyone grooves to the same beat.

2. **Competency Fit: Do you have the skills required for this position?**

   A heart for the mission is essential, but it's not enough. Competency Fit helps you evaluate whether someone has the right mix of technical skill, emotional intelligence, and leadership capacity to succeed in their role right now. This isn't about potential alone; it's about present readiness. These questions are designed to prompt honest dialogue in one-on-ones, helping you clarify strengths, surface gaps, and determine what support your team needs to thrive.

Evaluative Questions:

i. Do they have the job-relevant expertise required (skills and/or training)?

ii. Do they have the emotional intelligence needed for their role?

iii. Can they handle the workload, both in terms of hours and stress resilience?

iv. Do they have the leadership capacity your organization needs right now?

Example: One of the organizations we worked with developed the following four questions to spark a conversation with their staff during their one-on-ones.

i. **EQ:** When tensions rise or communication breaks down, how well do you help move the team toward trust, clarity, and calm?

ii. **Hard Skills:** Are you confident, and are others confident that you have the skills to consistently deliver excellent work in your core responsibilities?

iii. **Leadership:** In the areas you influence, do you consistently help move people, ideas, or projects forward in a way that builds trust and momentum?

iv. **Availability:** Given the season you're in and the needs of the role, are you available mentally, emotionally, and logistically with time to show up well and follow through?

Think of the Competency Fit like a member of a Formula 1 racing team pit crew. Every member needs the technical ability to execute their role in sync with the rest of the team under intense pressure, where every second counts. It's more than just being a technical specialist; the role must be fit for the crew as a whole.

3. **Compensation Fit: Does the compensation formula (money + meaning) equation of this organization work for you?**

   This section helps surface those internal tensions before they become exit interviews. It invites open conversations about both financial realities and purpose alignment so you can respond with clarity, not surprise.

   Evaluative Questions:

   i. Is the salary and benefits package genuinely sustainable for them?

   ii. Does the mission feed their sense of purpose enough to offset any pay gaps?

   iii. Might they leave in six months because they have outgrown the meaning or the money?

   Example: Here is how one organization we worked with built out this portion of the tool to spark a conversation with their staff during their one-on-ones.

   i. **Salary and Benefits:** $57k for beginning employees + benefits + generous time off + occasional weekend responsibilities + no staff direct reports + oversight of 2 volunteer teams.

   ii. **Passion:** Working directly with kids who need tutoring + responsible for increasing impact by adding two new schools per year to the tutoring program.

Picture the Compensation Fit like choosing a hometown. It's not just about the house (the salary); it's also about the community (the mission and its deeper meaning). If both aren't right, that person will move elsewhere. Nonprofits must ensure employees do not feel they are living in a place that fails to nourish their heart or their wallet.

Many of the organizations we have worked with use the helpful practice of sharing the concept of "Right Fit" with staff members during onboarding and continuing during reviews. Using this rubric is especially helpful for staff members who are struggling to determine not only whether they belong, but also how to invest in their growth and long-term success.

When you are aiming for development rather than correction, the conversation can be surprisingly rich. Team members become free to admit challenges they are facing that they wouldn't otherwise surface. A good supervisor responds to the need by taking practical steps, such as building their EQ (coaching, a reading list, and maybe even a mentor) or SQ (skill development and proficiency). Instead of feeling attacked, staff often walk away grateful, knowing where they stand and what they need to work on.

A Quickfire Assessment

Let's put the three parts of this tool together. Take a moment and give yourself a rating for each of the three categories: *Culture, Competency, and Compensation.*

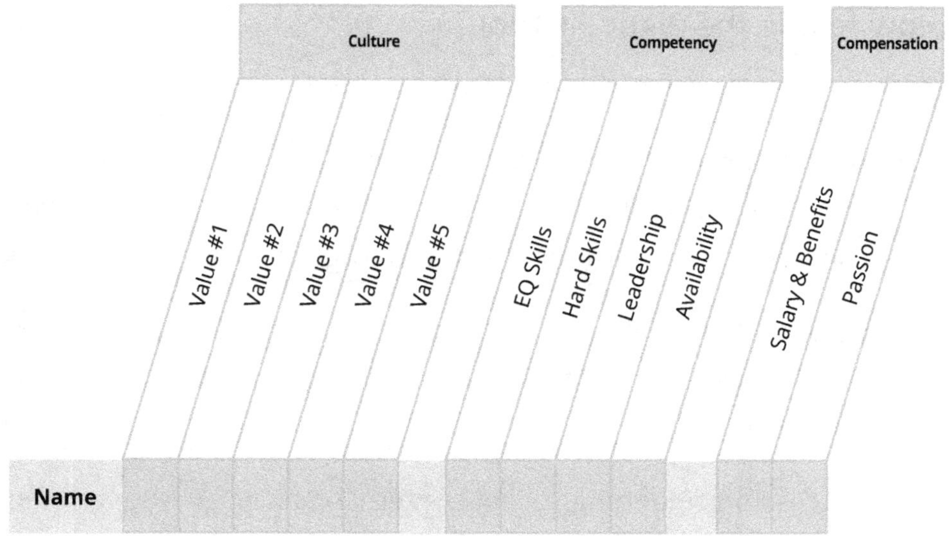

Use the simple traffic light system:

- Red (R) – Not meeting the standard
- Yellow (Y) – Borderline or inconsistent
- Green (G) – Fully meeting or exceeding the standard

Ask yourself:

- Where am I thriving?
- Where am I feeling shaky?
- What needs a deeper conversation?

What are the insights this quickfire assessment is revealing? This self-reflection can uncover quiet misalignments simmering under the surface or reveal strong alignment you have never clearly named. Either way, that clarity will help you move forward with confidence.

How to Use the Right Fit Tool

Here are ways to use the Right Fit Tool, including:

- **Annual Reviews:** Assess each team member's fit and performance using the Right Fit Tool to guide conversations around growth, contribution, and alignment with your organization.
- **Search & Hiring:** Use the unique questions generated by your customized Right Fit Tool to find the right fit for future team members.
- **Succession Planning:** Identify internal candidates who can step up and external candidates with whom you want to spend extra time in conversation.
- **Board Member Evaluation:** Clarify which board members are thriving and who may need redirection, re-engagement, or a respectful exit.
- **Volunteer Recruitment:** Select volunteers who not only want to serve but also align with your culture, mission, and expectations.
- **Conflict Resolution:** Diagnose friction points between staff members or between staff and managers.

Think of each application like using a Swiss Army Knife. One small tool can be used for many different purposes, from opening a bottle to tightening a screw. The Right Fit Tool is similarly versatile—whether you are deciding on a hire or supporting current staff.

People Tool #2: Board Tune-Up Tool

Thus far, we have focused on staff, but let's not forget your other core team: the board. As John Carver emphasizes in *Boards That Make a*

Difference, "When boards shift from micromanaging operational details to focusing on ends—bold, mission-oriented outcomes—they transform themselves into visionary bodies capable of leveraging an organization's full capacity. This shift is not just procedural, it is cultural." That cultural shift hinges on the board's understanding of its identity.

The Board Tune-Up Tool clarifies the current footprint of your board around five core areas:

1. **Type:** To what extent do members share a clear, common understanding of the board's identity and purpose?
2. **Needs:** To what extent does the board meet the organization's most pressing needs (e.g., fundraising, strategic guidance)?
3. **Commitment:** To what extent are members demonstrably committed to the mission of the organization?
4. **Activity:** To what extent can the board be mobilized quickly and reliably when the organization truly needs them?
5. **Alignment:** To what extent is the board aligned with staff and with one another around the organization's strategy and priorities?

We will not go into depth on each of these core areas. However, due to the critical nature of clarity needed around #1-Type, let's zoom in a little closer by asking the question: What type of Board do you need?

Board Type

Every nonprofit is legally required to have a board for IRS compliance, but a board's value can be so much more than bureaucratic oversight. Boards can bring strategic thinking, financial stewardship, professional networks, and much-needed encouragement to staff.

However, many nonprofits end up with hodgepodge boards composed of well-intentioned people who may have drastically different views of what the board should do.

If board members are not aligned on the board's function—governance, fundraising, advisory, or a blend of these—friction will inevitably follow. And if the ED or staff has a different idea of what the board should be doing than the board's own view? Watch out.

We have distilled the types of boards into five common board "identities", all having different types of governance responsibility:

1. Strategy Board

- **Definition:** Primarily responsible for oversight, policy creation, and ensuring legal compliance.
- **A Good Choice For:** Larger nonprofits that need strategic direction and high-level accountability.
- **A Poor Choice For:** Small nonprofits where day-to-day involvement from board members is needed.

2. Working Board

- **Definition:** Board members also serve in operational roles (e.g., as program staff volunteers).
- **A Good Choice For:** New or smaller nonprofits without enough full-time staff.
- **A Poor Choice For:** Larger nonprofits where the board might micromanage or meddle in staff roles.

3. Advisory Board

- **Definition:** Offers expert advice but does not hold legal fiduciary responsibility.

- **A Good Choice For:** Organizations that have a formal governance board already in place but need specialized input in law, finance, or programming.
- **A Poor Choice For:** Nonprofits who have yet to establish their governance board with actual fiduciary oversight.

4. **Fundraising Board**

- **Definition:** Members primarily serve to generate resources.
- **A Good Choice For:** Nonprofit whose most significant need is philanthropic connections.
- **A Poor Choice For:** Organizations that need the board to be highly involved in strategic decision-making.

5. **Honorary Board**

- **Definition:** High-profile individuals lending name recognition or moral support with minimal active duty.
- **A Good Choice For:** Large nonprofits with robust brand-building strategies.
- **A Poor Choice For:** Nonprofits that rely on the board for hands on involvement or oversight.

A small arts organization we worked with found itself with a mismatched board. They had designated themselves as a Fundraising Board. They drew up bylaws emphasizing 100% board giving, individual donor outreach, and corporate sponsorship. After a year of floundering, the Executive Director used the Board Tune-Up Tool and, through the conversation, discovered that only one board member had connections to high-capacity donors, corporate grants, or foundations. The rest were all local artists, passionate about art installations and community events, but not fundraisers. Essentially, most everyone was set up for failure.

Through the tool, they had a frank conversation: "We are a Fundraising Board in name, but not in reality." The result? They decided to pivot to an Advisory Board with a more modest, achievable fundraising requirement and build out a volunteer team to serve in this fundraising capacity. They also recruited two new board members whose networks aligned better with corporate sponsorships. This one change liberated the existing board members from feeling guilty or inadequate and positioned the nonprofit to thrive.

Don't assume the label matches reality. Many nonprofits label their board as an Advisory Board, but if half the members are also acting like staff, it's a Working Board in practice. Pinpoint your actual board identity (not just what it's called), then patiently shape it into the type of board that best serves your nonprofit.

The Spidergram

The Board Tune-Up Tool uses a simple spidergram to help you visualize and understand your *Board Footprint*. Each axis represents one of the Five Core Areas mentioned above (Type, Needs, Activity, Alignment, Commitment).

Directions for using the tool:

Step #1: Score your board on a scale of 1 to 100 on all of the Five Core Areas.

Step #2: Put a dot on the axis it belongs.

Step #3: Connect the dots.

Step #4: Shade in the area to see the shape of your board's performance.

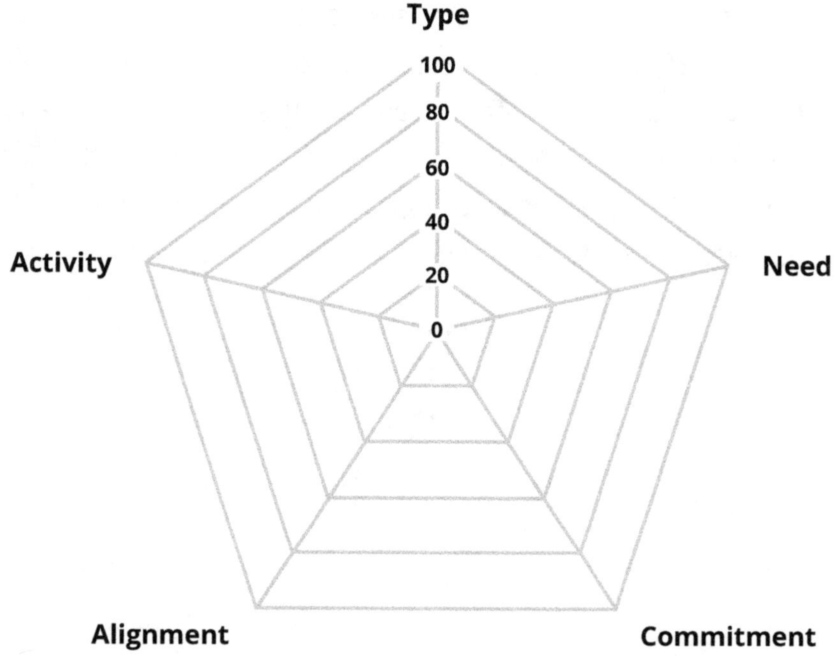

Step #5: Add your total scores together and divide by 5 to get an overall score. You now have a year-to-year score your board can use for ongoing discussion.

Step #6: Discuss with your Board, or Board Chair: What are the strengths, weaknesses, opportunities, and threats when you look at your Board footprint?

This isn't the *end* of the conversation. Here is where the conversation *begins*!

The shape of your spidergram might reveal glaring gaps. A board might be outstanding in "Type" and "Needs" but abysmal in "Alignment." That indicates they know what they are supposed to do and they do it well, yet they disagree on the big strategic picture.

A historic mental health nonprofit that serves teens in the Midwest held a board retreat. Half the board wanted to expand into telehealth; the other half felt that telehealth was impersonal and a betrayal of the organization's roots. Before we could tackle that strategy, we had them use the Board Tune-Up Tool. The result? Needs, Type, Activity, and Commitment all scored between 70 and 90. Alignment, however, scored a dismal 30.

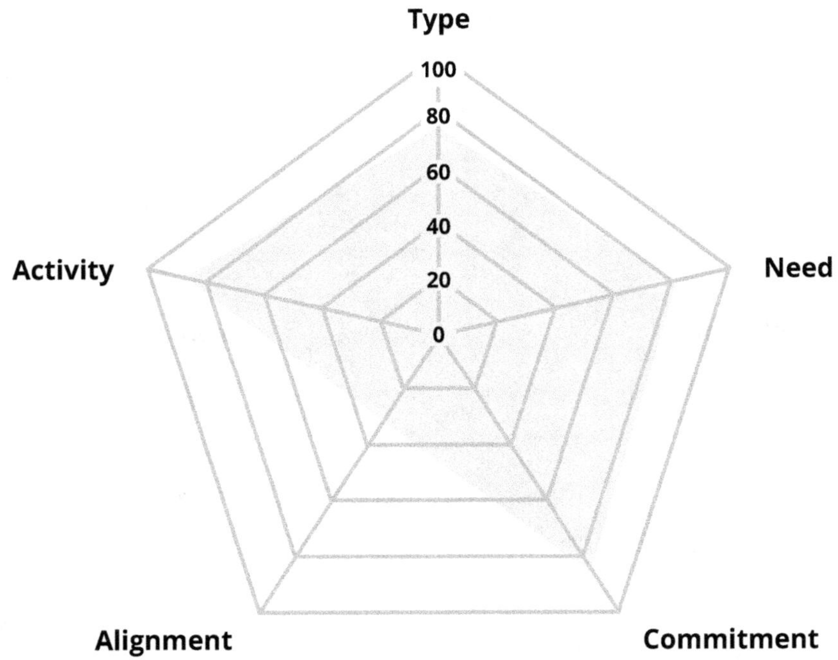

Once they saw the visual, no one could ignore the rift.

The ensuing conversation was honest, sometimes tense, but ultimately fruitful. They hammered out a pilot telehealth program specifically for rural communities that fit their mission's legacy and advanced it for modern times. By allowing the friction to surface in a structured way, they forged unity, rather than papering over the problem.

A Note on How to Use the Two Tools

Some tools we are giving you in this book are like hammers. You use them to build something solid, and once it's built, you are mostly done. Other tools are more like a compass. They don't "solve" a problem so much as help you find your bearings, start a meaningful journey, and keep you moving in the right direction. The latter is precisely how to use the Right Fit Tool and the Board Tune-Up Tool.

These tools do NOT exist to grade people or perfect your team. They are here to start a conversation by creating shared language, spark self-reflection, and make sure everyone is aiming toward the same destination. Used well, they help your team mature, not just perform.

They are meant to be revisited regularly and used rhythmically. You will never have a perfect staff member or board, but if you use the Right Fit Tool and the Board Tune-Up Tool once a year to guide an honest, hopeful conversation, you will move in the right direction. It's not about getting it right. It's about staying committed to getting better, together.

Conclusion

People are everything. They're the lifeblood of your nonprofit, the reason donors stay loyal, the ones delivering services, and the ambassadors for your cause in the community. Without them, there is no impact! No sophisticated strategy can compensate for people who feel forgotten, undervalued, or wrongfully placed. But when you invest in them by creating frameworks for honest feedback, encouraging annual "fit" evaluations, and keeping your board rowing in tandem, you cultivate an environment where everyone can flourish.

In this chapter, we focused on your people—the staff and the board.

In the next chapter, we will focus on the structures that people inhabit, because when you align the right individuals with the right structures, you create the kind of nonprofit that not only meets expectations but transforms entire communities for the better.

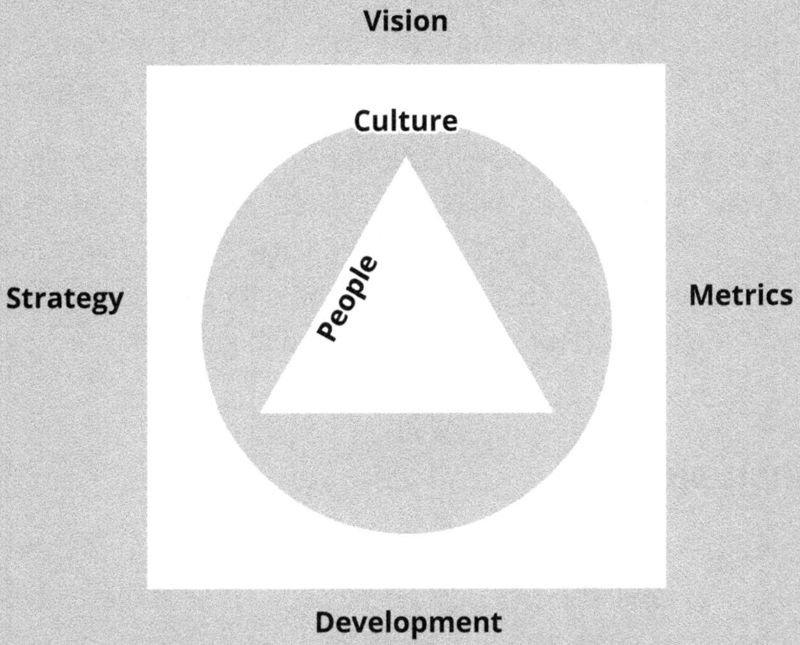

Vision

Culture

People

Strategy

Metrics

Development

59% of nonprofit employees cite their organizational structure as a primary reason for leaving their positions.

8

PEOPLE PART 2

As we write this book, we are working with a large mission-driven organization, and in the last few months, they've been experiencing a drop in team morale that is coming from an unexpected place.

By the nature of their mission, they have to place very large orders at a high dollar clip. Recently, the leader in charge of purchasing told us, "People are confused about how the process works. Everyone feels their need should come first, and the frustration is landing on our team. And more often...on me. Their concerns are real, but this isn't working."

As we dug in, we learned that the purchasing process was complicated because of their government partnerships and the many laws and regulations they had to follow. The team was running 3-4 months behind in purchasing, and their priorities kept shifting.

It's not about who holds power; it's about who is empowered.

It felt daunting, but they committed to a path from confusion to clarity. They built a simple, shared spreadsheet that anyone in the organization could view to see where a request stood and why. It explained what determined priority and offered a realistic timeframe for completion. *Most importantly, they named who was responsible for setting purchasing priorities and communicated that openly.*

Not everyone loved waiting for their item, of course. But the transparency eased tensions, took the pressure off the leader, and freed the team to focus on the work in front of them—moving ahead with a clear, agreed-upon list.

"Clear is kind," says Brené Brown. And the proper structure brings clarity to every role, every decision, every day. Those words may seem deceptively simple, but in the whirlwind of nonprofit work, it's a gift.

So, what if your organizational structure isn't a constraint, but an invitation to know what you are responsible for, and how to move the mission forward with clarity and confidence? After all:

> *59% of nonprofit employees cite their organizational structure as a primary reason for leaving their positions.*

In this chapter, we will deconstruct the myth that laissez-faire must be the norm in nonprofit structure and reconstruct a bold approach through two key tools:

- DARCI Framework clarifies decision-making and execution
- Org Chart Analyzer examines how your organizational structure accelerates or slows your impact

By the end, you will see that it's not about who holds power; it's about who is empowered. That's what clarity does: it creates the conditions for everyone to bring their best selves to the mission every day.

Who's in Charge?

Nonprofits can sometimes look like a vibrant patchwork quilt withlayers of staff, volunteers, partners, donors, and board members stitched together in pursuit of a mission. On a good day, it's a mosaic of talents and passions seamlessly united. On a not-so-good day, it can feel like a parade of well-intentioned chaos.

An organization we worked with found itself at a crossroads. A volunteer coalition was pushing for a new after-school program. Staff were calling for better community outreach. The board chair insisted the finance systems had to be overhauled. Everyone had energy. Everyone wanted progress. But no one was quite sure who was setting the direction.

Tension mounted like helium in a balloon, ready to burst the moment someone asked the inevitable: "Who is making all the decisions around here?"

That question is an understandable one. Traditionally, we assume that a single figure—the CEO, the Executive Director, the board chair, the project lead—must hold the reins. But nonprofits rarely concentrate power in one person, both for bigger and day-to-day decisions.

To get the correct answer, we have to ask the right question. So is the question really, "Who's in charge?" Or is there a more precise and nuanced way to ask it?

Who's in Charge of What?

When the stakes are high, asking, "Who's in charge?" rarely illuminates the whole picture. A far more powerful question is, "Who's in charge of what?" By breaking down responsibilities and decision points, we recognize that different roles wield different types of authority. One person might be the official decision-maker for a project, while another is the subject-matter expert responsible for day-to-day tasks. Others may be consulted for niche expertise, and still others merely need to be informed about changes and project progress.

Picture this scenario: You are racing to launch a new youth-mentorship initiative that will pair high school volunteers with at-risk middle school students. The program is both urgent and vital. These kids need immediate support, and it aligns perfectly with your organization's mission. The board is eager, the staff is excited, and you even have a donor who's offered to match funding if you launch quickly.

However, there's a snag: Who gets to decide if you should partner with the local school board? Is that a board decision or something your Executive Director can greenlight? And if the ED can greenlight it, who's truly accountable for the outcome: your program director or your operations manager? Is the ED doing the work if they made the decision and are accountable, or is that someone else? Plus, do you need input from your new volunteer council, or do you simply inform them after decisions are made? (Overwhelmed yet?) With multiple stakeholders (each with a role, a voice, and a vested interest), failing to define who does what can stall progress or create friction.

"Who's in charge?" rarely illuminates the whole picture. A far more powerful question is, "Who's in charge of what?"

Nonprofits tend to get stuck in a decision loop with new projects. They gather people in a flurry of good intentions, discuss the possibilities, and then spin in a swirl of confusion about final say and next steps. Meanwhile, kids who need mentorship are sitting on waitlists.

Is there a way to prevent getting stuck in the dreaded decision loop?

Tool #1: The DARCI Framework

DARCI is a roles-and-responsibilities framework adapted from the RACI model developed by the Project Management Institute (PMI) in the 1970s. While the acronym may not roll off the tongue, its impact is undeniable. Nonprofits often find DARCI to be a game-changer because it reflects the complex reality of shared responsibility. In environments where power, accountability, and expertise are dispersed across staff, volunteers, donors, and board members, this tool brings clarity to decision-making. It helps teams move forward with alignment and confidence.

Here's how the framework breaks down:

- **D – Decision Maker:** The person (or group) with final authority. They say "go" or "no-go" for a particular project or for day-to-day processes.
- **A – Accountable:** The individual who is ultimately accountable for the outcomes; the "buck stops" with this person.
- **R – Responsible:** The doer(s). The individuals responsible for executing tasks that ensure steady progress.
- **C – Consulted:** Those who provide input, expertise, or critical feedback. They do not make the final call, but can influence decisions.
- **I – Informed:** Individuals or parties who need to be kept in the loop. They do not shape the decision or do the work, but they require updates.

Organizational Function	D Decision Maker	A Accountable	R Responsible	C Consulted	I Informed
Fundraising					
Function 2					
Function 3					
Etc.					

Using the DARCI Framework – Step by Step

Step 1#: Make a list of the 6-7 most important functions of work your nonprofit executes

Examples:

- Fundraising
- Budget
- Programming
- Volunteer Training

Step #2: Complete the DARCI Framework for This Function

For the purpose of this exercise, lets use the function of Fundraising.

- Decision Maker: Who makes the final decision on fundraising strategy?
- Accountable: Who is accountable to ensure the strategy is executed and goals are achieved?
- Responsible: Who is involved in the workflow, what are they doing, and when are the deadlines?
- Consulted: Who do we need to shape the fundraising, get feedback from, and what's the process for getting it?
- Informed: Who do we need to keep in the loop as the strategy moves forward, and when it is completed?

Step #3: Determine the Pertinent Subcategories That Correlate with Each of the Primary Functions

- Every function that warrants a DARCI buildout will have subcategories. There is no prescribed number of subcategories for each function.

- Example: Under the Fundraising function, you will likely have a subcategory entitled, "Meeting with high-net-worth individuals."

Step #4: For Each Subcategory, Fill Out the DARCI Framework

- Decision Maker: Who makes the final decision on the high-net-worth individual initiative?
- Accountable: Who is accountable for its outcomes?
- Responsible: Who is involved in the workflow, what are they doing, and when are the deadlines?
- Consulted: Who do we need to shape how we meet with high-net-worth individuals, get feedback from, and what's the process for getting it?
- Informed: Who do we need to keep in the loop as the strategy moves forward and when it is completed?

	D Decision Maker	**A** Accountable	**R** Responsible	**C** Consulted	**I** Informed
Function: Fundraising	Development Director	Development Director	Development Team	Fundraising Consultants & Executive Director	Rest of Staff
Tactics for Cultivating Prospects with High Net Worth	Development Director	Executive Director	Executive Director & Development Director	Board	Board & Staff

DARCI Framework Coaching Tips

Here are a few helpful places that you can apply this tool:

1. **Use DARCI at the start of a new project.**

   Consistently following this pattern will help you set the entire team up for success. It removes guesswork. It minimizes "decision by committee" fiascos in the middle of projects and ensures that staff and volunteers are not left to interpret ambiguous signals about authority.

2. **Use DARCI. for routine functions within the organization.**

   These can range from basic external communications strategies to cross-departmental communication. This too will head off confusion, anxiety, and dropped balls because it extends clarity into everyday operations.

3. **Use DARCI for most of what you do, but not all of what you do.**

   We have seen this tool used to micromanage rather than to bring clarity. Typically, there will only be 6-7 categories and 30-40 subcategories. Any more than that and it can create a "Big Brother" culture.

4. **Include every name in each function and subcategory.**

   This is important because it forces a level of specificity that prevents too many people from being involved, and thus defeats the goal of "decision by committee." The magic is getting the "right" people involved at every level, not necessarily everyone at every level.

5. **Make DARCI visible to all the staff, volunteers, and board members.**

   Don't let the framework live in a silo. For it to actually shape decision-making and clarify roles, it needs to be accessible and visible across the organization. Post it in the shared team Google Drive, embed it in project templates, and walk through it during staff and board training. Visibility transforms DARCI from a behind-the-scenes tool into a shared language.

6. **Include the DARCI Framework itself as a function.**

   While it may seem obvious, it's worth noting that someone in your organization needs to be responsible for ensuring that every appropriate function and subcategory has been built out and followed correctly.

By nature, this is not a complicated tool. However, it does require a concentrated level of work and discussion to achieve clarity on your organization's most critical functions. It will help avoid confusion and reduce delays caused by overlapping duties or unclear expectations, while ensuring that everyone understands their place in the workflow, aligns resources, promotes efficient execution, and provides helpful feedback.

A community arts nonprofit we worked with was recently planning a children's theater festival. Two well-meaning board members started drafting the festival program and lining up guests, thinking they were helping. The staff froze because of the influence and authority wielded by the board members. Obviously, this frustrated the staff because the well-meaning board was overstepping into their operational domain. After much confusion, they realized no one had assigned the Decider or the Responsible roles. Everyone was swirling around, stepping on each other's toes, believing they were championing the cause.

Wisely, they paused amid the chaos and quickly implemented DARCI. After doing so, they discovered that the marketing manager was the Decider for festival materials, and the communications director was Accountable and Responsible for creating and final approvals.

The Executive Director needed to be Consulted, and the board members simply needed to be Informed about big-picture event details. That single piece of clarity turned a chaotic scramble into a smooth production.

Once you have clarified roles and responsibilities for projects and everyday processes, it's time to address the architectural structure of your nonprofit.

Tool #2: The Org Chart Analyzer

Most nonprofit teams have passionate people, but many organizations and their staff are unclear about roles within the overall structure. The Org Chart Analyzer helps clarify who's on the bus, who's in the right seat, and what changes are needed to align your people with your mission.

The Org Chart Analyzer addresses two critical questions:

1. Does our structure help or hinder clarity?
2. What changes should be made to support our next stage of growth?

Think of your nonprofit's org chart as a blueprint of empowerment. It's like a living map where terrain shifts as you grow and pivot. If DARCI is the hammer that helps you nail down specific roles for a project, the Org Chart Analyzer is the compass that enables you to navigate the big picture over time, so you are not lost when the inevitable storms of change roll in.

In the previous section, we mentioned that some tools, like DARCI, must be used regularly (weekly) to achieve clarity. Other tools serve more as periodic check-ins, like The Org Chart Analyzer (once or twice a year).

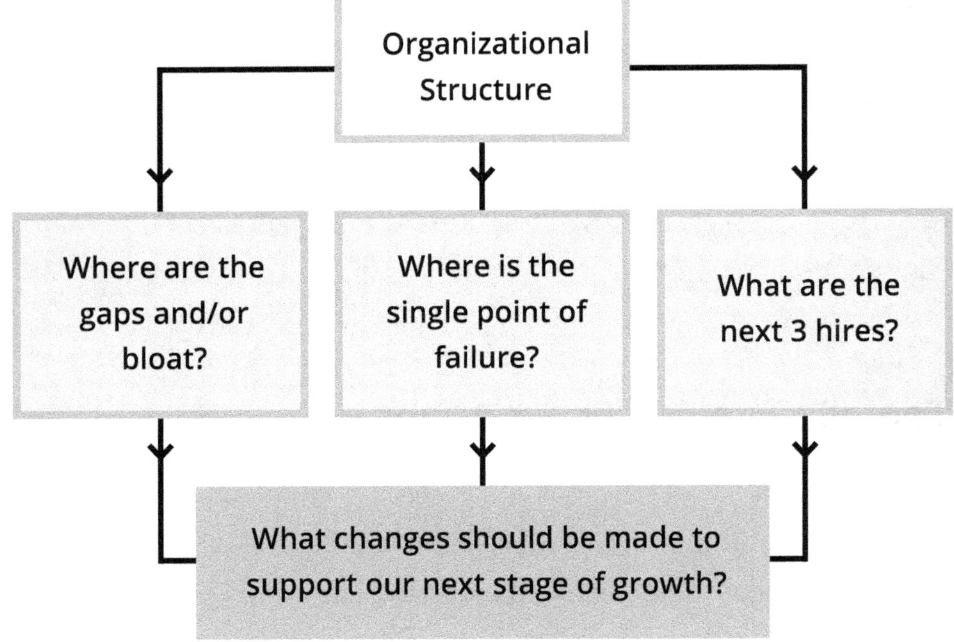

The Org Chart Analyzer

While it is a deceptively simple set of questions, it opens critical discussions about mission alignment, capacity, and sustainability.

1. **Where are there gaps and/or bloat in our structure?**

   This question helps you assess both under-resourced areas and overbuilt segments of the organization. Gaps might include missing roles, unclear responsibilities, or teams stretched too thin to deliver quality outcomes. Bloat, on the other hand, could show up as duplicated efforts, unnecessary layers of decision-making, or legacy roles that no longer serve the mission.

2. **Where is the single point of failure?**

   This question helps nonprofits identify areas where a process, relationship, or outcome hinges too heavily on one individual, vendor, or system. If that person leaves, or that system crashes, does everything fall apart? Pinpointing these fragile dependencies allows leaders to build redundancy, share knowledge, and create backup plans to avoid derailing the mission.

3. **What are the next three hires (or roles) we need?**

   This question prompts leaders to zoom out from current job descriptions and think strategically about the future: What expertise, leadership, or capacity would most strengthen our mission in the next 12 -18 months? Answering this will define your next critical hires by considering both urgency and importance.

4. **What changes should be made to support our next stage of growth?**

   This question is about prioritization and focus. After identifying gaps, points of failure, and strategic hiring needs, it's tempting to overhaul too much at once. But real growth requires disciplined change.

   This prompt encourages leaders to name no more than three specific changes to unlock the next phase of effectiveness. These could be structural shifts (e.g., decentralizing decision-making), role adjustments (e.g., clarifying supervisory oversight), or capacity investments (e.g., implementing a shared services model).

These simple questions, used at least once a year, will ensure your organization can always bear the load of your mission by being proactive rather than reactive.

There Is No Such Thing as a Perfect Org Chart

In *High Performance Nonprofit Organizations: Managing Upstream for Greater Impact*, Christine Letts, William Ryan, and Allen Grossman articulate an important idea:

> "Fix upstream issues to prevent downstream crises. It's far more effective to strengthen the internal systems of leadership and accountability before external pressures force hasty decision-making."

That's precisely what you do when you analyze your org chart: you handle potential bottlenecks (upstream issues) before they deplete staff morale or hamper outcomes (downstream crises).

Let's put this into context with an example. A nonprofit called GrantFinder set out to bring FinTech innovation to small and medium-sized nonprofits, making it easier for them to find and win available grants. They launched with a lean structure: a founder/executive director, a tech lead, and a small but passionate volunteer base. They had early success, riding a wave of interest from philanthropic funders who saw the potential in bridging technology and grassroots missions.

A year in, they realized their rapid growth had outpaced their structure. Each staff member was wearing too many hats. Volunteers felt underutilized. The board, which had initially been hands-on, suddenly found itself unsure whether to continue driving product strategy or revert to a more traditional governance model. Tensions spiked when a major philanthropic partner asked for a product pivot, requiring more time from the already overextended tech lead. Their simple org chart looked like this:

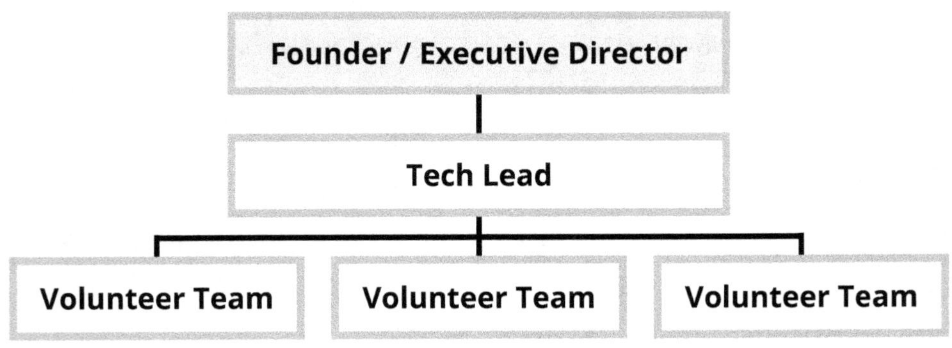

That's when they pulled out the Org Chart Analyzer and asked four questions. This is how they answered those questions:

1. **Where are the gaps or bloat?** They noticed they had no one dedicated to customer support (a gap), and their tech lead was overwhelmed with admin tasks that could be automated (a sign of bloat in how tasks were assigned).

2. **Where is the single point of failure?** The tech lead, ironically. If this person left or burned out, the entire product line would be at risk.

3. **What are the next three hires?** They needed a solutions architect to relieve the tech lead, a customer support lead, and a part-time volunteer manager to free up the volunteer coordinator for more strategic community-building.

4. **What changes should be made to support our next stage of growth?** They mapped out the new structure, and here is what they decided:

    - Tech Lead: Remains essential, but they needed to hire a solutions architect to share the load.

    - Customer Support Lead: They elevated the volunteer coordinator's role to manage a small team of paid interns, ensuring that nonprofits using their platform had round-the-clock support.

    - Volunteer Manager: They shifted from purely administrative tasks to strategic volunteer engagement, especially for marketing the platform.

Here is how these changes looked with their new org chart:

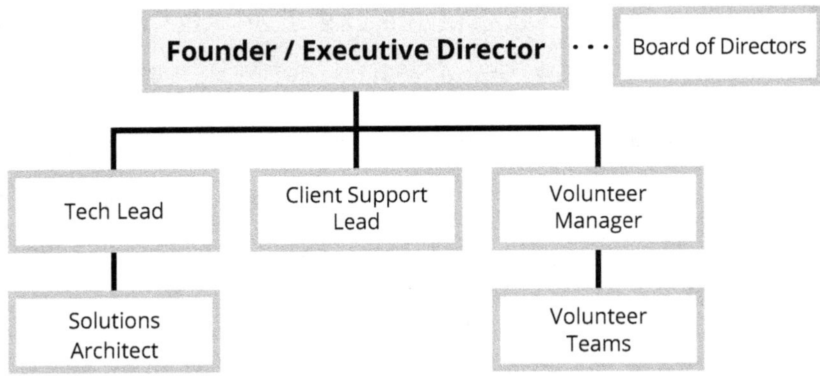

Using the Org Chart Analyzer as a Compass

There is no perfect org chart because people and priorities change. When you become too rigid—straining to achieve or clinging to an ideal structure—you risk stagnation. But by periodically reviewing your org chart, you can identify challenges and opportunities before they become crises.

Most organizations think the org chart is about "who reports to whom." More helpfully, an org chart is a statement of who you are empowering to make decisions and who may be disempowered. The biggest surprise for many nonprofits is discovering how often they under-empower the very people they depend on most (like program managers or volunteer coordinators) by burying them three levels down. The epiphany that you might be structurally disempowering your talent can be the difference between incremental progress and explosive impact.

People vs. Structure?

Do people serve the structure, or does the structure serve the people?

While this question may seem obvious to some, it can be confusing for organizations going through change. It's essential to keep this principle in mind: *Structures only exist to help people win in their roles, not the other way around. If you find that your people exist to serve the structure, that's the tail wagging the dog.*

An organization loses significantly when a retired teacher, eager to tutor at her local literacy nonprofit, becomes frustrated with a complicated structure and says, "I didn't sign up to navigate bureaucracy. I just want to help kids read!" When volunteer systems are clunky, communication is murky, and role boundaries are ignored, it's only a matter of time before fatigue outweighs motivation. It's crucial to systematically ensure that your structure serves your people, not the other way around.

Conclusion

We opened this chapter with a quote from Brené Brown, "Clear is kind." And the right structure brings clarity to every role, every decision, every day. This is a guiding principle for nonprofits that often operate in fluid, high-need environments. Whether you use the DARCI tool to define decision-making or the Org Chart Analyzer to uncover structural blind spots, the goal remains the same: *empower people to do their best work.*

Neither of these tools is a quick fix. Both require intentionality, a willingness to question old assumptions, and above all, the courage to place people and mission at the center of every structural decision.

As you move forward, keep an empathetic eye on how these frameworks affect morale. Clarity doesn't leave folks guessing or stewing in uncertainty. It honors their time, respects their intelligence, and affirms their contributions. In turn, they'll feel more engaged, more aligned with your mission, and more committed to driving the impact for which you strive.

Vision

Culture

People

Systems

Strategy

Metrics

Development

26% of the average nonprofit staffer's day is wasted on inefficient tasks.

9

SYSTEMS

Don't skip this chapter! (That's a foreboding way to kick things off, isn't it?)

For many, a discussion about building repeatable systems might sound... well...uninspiring. After all, you were called to a mission, not a checklist. But time and again, the nonprofits that steadily advance their Vision aren't just passionate—they're *lightly* structured. They have discovered that the path to consistent impact is paved with intentional, repeatable processes that allow staff and volunteers to do their best work, free from the frustration of reinventing the wheel.

Think of it this way: People run systems, and systems run organizations.

People run systems, and systems run organizations.

Believe it or not, the key to making your mission more achievable and your day-to-day life more peaceful often lies in well-crafted, simple processes that everyone consistently uses. We have found this component of the Impact Operating System to be the most overlooked by organizations.

Be assured, it will be worth your while.

In this chapter, we will discuss:

- Why Simple, Repeatable Systems Matter to Nonprofits
- The 7VIP Tool
- Examples of Very Important Processes
- Best Practices and Coaching Tips For Integrating Your 7VIPs

Why Simple Repeatable Systems Matter to Nonprofits

Picture this: You are in the middle of a busy fundraising season. A major foundation has requested a grant proposal, which is good news. Actually, it's great news! However, the staff member who was responsible for grant writing left for another job out of state and wiped their computer before turning it in (including the proposal template). So, you have to start over. Google and ChatGPT promise to be your allies, but you quickly discover there are endless versions, each with different formatting, and the foundation has given you no directions. You then discover your metrics are outdated and your yearly budgets are mismatched. Oh, and by the way, you have to run the volunteer training at 3 pm, and you have a board meeting at 6 pm.

The path to consistent impact is paved with intentional, repeatable processes that allow staff and volunteers to do their best work, free from the frustration of reinventing the wheel.

Anyone ready to climb into bed and pull the covers over your head?

Unfortunately, this scenario, and others like it, are commonplace. The problem is not effort. It is the absence of simple, shared processes everyone can follow.

> *A staggering 26% of the average nonprofit employee's work-day is lost to unnecessary or inefficient tasks.*

Over a year, that adds up to countless hours and dollars that could have gone directly toward advancing the mission. The hard truth? No amount of heart or passion can patch serious operational gaps. Without streamlined systems, even the most committed teams end up burned out, frustrated, and stretched too thin. And eventually, it's not just morale that suffers, it's the mission itself.

However, clear processes can convert chaos into breakthrough.

Research shows that nonprofits with well-documented, repeatable processes experience significantly fewer volunteer departures. In our experience, that amounts to about 60% fewer staff turnovers every two years. That's not a benign statistic, it's mindblowing! Everyone wants to reduce burnout, build more consistent programs, and expand their talent pipeline.

It might seem counterintuitive that a system can spark such passion and unleash creativity. When your team knows exactly how to execute tasks, they can channel their energy into problem-solving and innovation rather than wrestling with disorganization. People truly thrive in structured freedom—enough process to guide them, paired with enough flexibility that allows them to excel. Systems foster the stability your mission deserves.

If you're reading this book, it's because you passionately want to see the mission of your nonprofit advance. You are striving for impact, and you know better than almost anyone else: *Avoidable chaos is one of the most significant challenges facing nonprofits today.*

The 7VIP Tool

Very Important Process (VIP) = a repeatable workflow that directly supports your nonprofit's mission by saving time, reducing confusion, and increasing consistency.

A VIP is the operational heartbeat of your nonprofit: the 20% of your daily operational tasks that yield 80% of your organization's critical operational results. It's the engine that keeps your mission running smoothly. Each VIP typically involves multiple steps, stakeholders, and a predictable order of actions. It's vital because, without it, your mission stalls.

The point isn't the Very Important Process. The point is that if you don't attend to them, their absence stalls the mission itself.

You know you have a VIP when it is dead center in the bullseye:

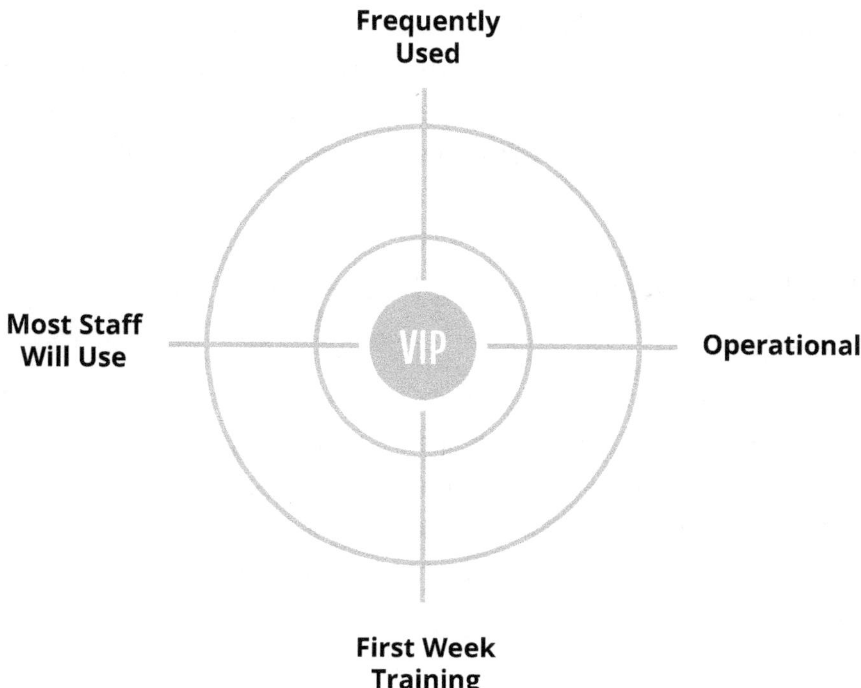

Operational: This is not a strategic concept. It's a hands-on, nuts-and-bolts process that keeps your organization's engine running smoothly. (*Example:* How to keep track of expenses and file an expense report. It's foundational, repeatable, and directly tied to making sure you stay IRS compliant.)

Frequently Used: This is a process that shows up in your organization's daily or weekly rhythm. It's not occasional, it's constant. (*Example:* Submitting and approving time-off requests. It happens regularly and affects daily scheduling and team coverage.)

Widely Used by Most Staff: It's not limited to one role or department. This process touches the majority of your team and ensures alignment across functions. (*Example:* Internal communication protocol. When do you use Slack or Teams for updates and urgent messages versus email or another communication medium?)

First-Week Training-Worthy: It's essential enough that you train new hires immediately, because getting it wrong could create confusion or delays. (*Example:* How to log client or program data in your CRM or database. Getting this right early ensures quality reporting and continuity of care.)

What Are the Wins of Having Repeatable VIPs?

1. Time Saved

By capturing a proven sequence of steps, you can stop trying to reinvent the wheel. You eliminate the "sideways energy" that drains staff capacity as they scramble to remember who's supposed to do what or where the latest version of the budget is stored. Your team's day-to-day gets smoother, and time can be reclaimed for more strategic, high-impact work.

2. Quality Increase

When processes are documented and consistently followed, the result is a significant improvement in quality. Whether it's volunteer training or donor engagement, standardized methods guarantee a more predictable (and usually better) outcome. When everyone is singing from the same sheet of music, those you are attempting to serve get your best.

3. Risk Mitigation

A well-defined, consistently followed process acts like an insurance policy against costly missteps. When procedures are vague or left to memory, critical details fall through the cracks. Repeatable processes minimize the risk of reputational damage or legal exposure by ensuring everyone understands expectations and how to meet them. They also create a safety net during transitions, allowing your organization to remain steady when staff changes or crises arise.

We worked with a well-known organization that supports impoverished children around the world. A crucial part of their donor retention strategy involved personalized letters connecting each donor's support to a child's real-life story. For most of their global programs, this worked brilliantly. But there was one country where donor retention had dropped off a cliff, and no one could figure out why.

When we sat down with them, we discovered that their local team in this country had been skipping a deceptively essential yet straightforward step: mailing the letters (it was much more complex than this, but this was the net result). It seems almost too basic to miss, right? But in the shuffle of cultural nuances, translation barriers, and administrative hiccups, it slipped through the cracks. The result? Donors were not receiving those heartfelt notes that forged a tangible bond between sponsor and child.

Within a month of solidifying that VIP and ensuring letters arrived, retention rates in that country soared back up, and donors felt the personal connection they had been longing for. Sometimes, it's the smallest gap in a system that makes the most significant difference.

Again. The point isn't the VIP. The point was that the lack of the VIP was blocking the effectiveness of the mission.

Structure That Lets Passion Grow

In the nonprofit world, there is often a stigma that if you systematize too much, you risk losing the "human touch." While it's true that passion cannot be fully captured on a flowchart, it can also be messy. Yet it's also true that processes, by nature, do not extinguish passion.

Well-designed and implemented processes create a sturdy channel that allows passion to flow farther, faster. When a nonprofit has documented VIPs for training volunteers, reimbursing expenses, or launching an event, it provides the ability to respond to a community's needs more effectively. This is precisely why Verne Harnish said in *Scaling Up*, "Routine sets you free." That "freedom" means you can pivot quicker when emergencies arise, because you are not constantly wrestling with day-to-day confusion or chaos.

As someone leading an organization, what you're trying to hit for each staff member is the *70/30 Rule*. There is no job on planet Earth where someone loves the daily or weekly tasks of their role 100% of the time. The sweet spot tends to be that at least 70% of their time is spent on tasks that energize them, where they find joy and feel genuinely good at their job. But the reality is that a chunk of time for every role will include things they wouldn't necessarily choose, but that's the nature of being an adult with a job! What the 7VIPs will do is actively serve you, your organization, and each team member to decrease the number of operational tasks that drain life and energy rather than give it.

VIPs are not asking everyone to do everything perfectly. You're asking everyone to do seven things with remarkable consistency.

Think of it like growing grapes in a vineyard. The trellis (a simple wooden framework) helps direct and support the plant. With just a little bit of direction, this delicate, organic plant can grow in the right direction and have all the support it needs when the fruit arrives. Similarly, when you provide just enough structure through simple systems, passion is free to grow and produce fruit.

Choosing Your 7VIPs

The 7VIP Tool is your nonprofit's blueprint for consistent excellence in your seven most used and most critical operational processes that you document, hone, and lean on. This tool narrows your focus to what matters most, rather than attempting to systematize every nook and cranny at once.

As previously emphasized, nonprofit leaders often grapple with the tension of giving people freedom to innovate and establishing accountability to drive impact. The 7VIP approach attempts to strike that balance. It identifies where you need uniformity and crystal-clear steps, while still leaving room in other areas for spontaneity, creativity, and personal flair.

Filing an expense report is required of every employee. That can take 20 minutes or 2 hours. A VIP will help you make it 20 minutes, giving you 100 more minutes to spend on the things you care about far more in your job than filing an expense report.

The reality is that no organization can be a well-oiled machine everywhere, especially nonprofits that rely on volunteers and frequently shifting priorities based on donor or community needs. Yet you can be a well-oiled machine in your seven most pivotal processes. Once honed, this will provide more margin to make a deeper impact in your community.

VIPs are not about asking everyone to do everything perfectly. You're asking everyone to do seven things with remarkable consistency.

To live out the power of the 7VIPs, take the following steps:

Step #1: Identify Your VIPs

To create your 7VIPs, you first need to identify which processes truly matter the most. A helpful principle here is the Pareto Principle—the idea that 20% of your efforts produce 80% of your results. In nonprofit terms, think about which processes, if improved, would yield the most significant positive impact on operations and save the most amount of time and removal of chaos. Another approach is to ask: "Where am I, or my team, spending a disproportionate amount of time?" or "Which tasks, if bungled, create the biggest headaches or missed opportunities?"

To illustrate possibilities, here are ten examples of repeatable processes that are standard in nonprofits that meet the qualifications of both important and frequent:

1. **HR Process for Staff**

   How you search, find, hire, orient, manage, review, promote, retain, and, if needed, fire people.

2. **Accounting Process**

   The flow and management of all incoming and outgoing funds.

3. **Volunteer Recruitment**

   Consistent steps to attract qualified, enthusiastic volunteers for your programs and events.

4. **Volunteer Training**

   Steps to onboard and equip new and existing volunteers so they can confidently serve.

5. **High Net Worth Donor Acquisition**

   The approach to identifying, cultivating, and stewarding major donors who can accelerate your mission.

6. **Expense Reports**

   A streamlined method for staff to submit and get reimbursed for expenses, ensuring transparency.

7. **Program Outcome Tracking**

   How you gather, log, and report metrics on program results, including data collection and analysis.

8. **Communications & Branding Approval**

   A system to ensure newsletters, social posts, websites, collateral material (etc.) align with your brand and core message.

9. **Fundraising Event Execution**

   A structured timeline for planning, marketing, executing, and debriefing fundraising events of all sizes.

10. **Board Engagement Process**

    How your board is informed, involved, and accountable, including meeting cycles and follow-up.

We are giving you ten examples, *but we are not saying, "Pick seven from this list."* We are simply showing these to help you better understand what might qualify as a VIP for you. You will want to create your own list that will yield the greatest return on time, improved quality, or risk mitigation. Your seven repeatable VIPs create a cohesive operational system.

Step #2: Document with Clarity

Once you identify your 7VIPs, you will need to document them. Nonprofits often shortchange this step or skip it altogether. They say, "We already know how to do it." Sure, but there's a big difference between 'institutional memory' living in your program director's head and a structured, bullet-pointed blueprint your entire team can access. "A process is only as strong as its consistent application; accountability ensures everyone follows the system," says Gino Wickman in *Traction*. And consistent application hinges on clarity. *If you want everyone to get to the same destination, they need the same map.*

If you are leading a school field trip, you don't want everyone relying on directions like, "I think we make a left at the big oak tree." Instead, you want a well-labeled itinerary so all students can find their way without wandering off. The same logic applies to your core processes.

Why does clarity win? Because it fosters trust, both internally among staff/volunteers and externally among donors and clients. If every staff member has to guess how to handle expense reimbursements, mistakes multiply (and your accountant will quit!). But if the steps are simple and published, each request is processed smoothly, no matter who is in the finance seat that day. It frees you from constantly answering "How do I do this again?" or dealing with reimbursements that arrive in the wrong format.

Here is a brief sample documented process for Volunteer Recruitment. Notice how it's broken into steps, each with sub-bullets, but also notice how the entire VIP can fit on one page. You are not writing a manual for the process, you're giving a trip-tick:

Sample Volunteer Recruitment Process

1. **Define Volunteer Role & Requirements**
    - Identify the specific needs (e.g., tutoring, admin help, marketing).
    - Determine time commitments, skill sets, and location requirements.
    - Collaborate with program leads to finalize the volunteer position description.

2. **Draft Recruitment Materials**
    - Update the volunteer role description in plain, friendly language.
    - Create or revise any digital or print collateral (flyers, social media posts).
    - Ensure branding meets nonprofit guidelines (Communications & Branding Approval Process).

3. **Pass on, Post & Promote**
   - Post the volunteer opportunity on your website, social media, and volunteer match sites.
   - Share internally with staff and board members who might recruit from their networks.
   - Track leads using a simple spreadsheet or CRM to avoid losing potential volunteers.
4. **Screen & Interview**
   - Receive and log inquiries (name, contact info, area of interest) into CRM.
   - Perform a brief phone or video screening, if needed.
   - Schedule in-person or virtual interviews for roles that require in-depth assessment.
5. **Selection & Onboarding**
   - Communicate clearly with chosen and unchosen volunteers about next steps.
   - Provide relevant paperwork, including background checks (if applicable).
   - Direct them to the Volunteer Training Process for orientation details.
6. **Feedback & Follow-Up**
   - Send a welcome email or letter that reaffirms your mission and volunteer expectations.
   - Assign a volunteer coordinator or staff buddy.
   - Collect feedback from new volunteers to refine your recruitment process over time.

Coaching Tip:

Invite multiple voices into your 7VIP Documentation. Beware of having the person closest to the work create the process in isolation. Gather a small group to review and shape the steps. The goal is not to capture one person's habits, but to create the best version of the process for now and for what's ahead, built from a shared/multiple/diverse point of view.

How to Document Your 7VIPs:

- **Accessibility:** If your process doc is hidden on a random staffer's laptop, it's useless. Store it on a shared drive, an organizational wiki, or an internal website your team can easily locate. On our ImpactHub platform, the main menu includes a Knowledge Base that contains all the documents you create through this process, including the 7VIPs.
- **Format:** Use booklets, e-courses, pamphlets, even simple PDFs. Pick whatever resonates with your team (and consider using multiple formats).Make sure it's user-friendly; add visuals or flowcharts where appropriate.
- **Regular Review:** Beware of becoming a slave to the processes you create. One way to avoid that is to regularly review and update them (quarterly, semi-annually, or annually) to ensure they are serving their intended purpose.
- **Simplicity:** Keep them concise. As Atul Gawande says in *The Checklist Manifesto*, "Complex tasks demand simple checks to avoid mistakes." A 100-page manual will just collect dust. Aim for brevity with clear headings, bullets, or short checklists.

Step #3: Train with Regularity

Training propels your 7VIPs from theoretical documents into real-world success. Too often, leaders assume that once a process is spelled out, voilà, the job is done! But people don't magically absorb written procedures. They need to practice, ask questions, and see how the steps work in context.

One of the biggest pitfalls we often see is mistaking "teaching" for "training." Teaching is the simple transfer of information, like handing someone a user manual and ensuring they can use the manual. Training, by contrast, involves demonstration, repetition, feedback, and real-world application. It's the difference between reading about how to ride a bike and riding a bicycle with someone running alongside, guiding you.

To truly embed your 7VIPs, you need at least two training approaches:

1. **Onboarding New Staff and Volunteers**

    - Hold an orientation module that covers each VIP your new team member needs to know.
    - Include practical exercises or role-playing if relevant (e.g., how to use your CRM, how to greet volunteers at an event).
    - Pair them with an experienced staff member for a designated amount of time who exemplifies mastery of the process.

2. **Introducing the 7VIPs Requires Ongoing Training for Current Staff and Volunteers**

    - Conduct brief refresher sessions, perhaps annually. Celebrate folks who adopt the processes well, and graciously challenge those who veer off track.

- If you are introducing new processes, frame them as enhancements that save time or reduce errors, so they quickly see the benefit.

A nonprofit manager sheepishly told us she worked hard to find, purchase, and install new fundraising software and attempted to "train" staff on it by emailing them a 20-page PDF manual! (Note: This should elicit a chuckle because, although it was excellent work, not a soul in the world would read that much material on software!) A few weeks later, she reported the new system had been causing nonstop headaches. Not exactly surprising, right?

Coaching Tip:

Do the good work of documenting with clarity, but also schedule (and require) training with regularity. Invest the energy to ensure these sessions are lively and creative so that no one is conveniently "sick" on those days because they abhor those meetings. If possible, feed people and give them gift cards. Make these sessions hands-on and interactive, include Q&A, and, for the love of humanity, keep them brief! Training emails vanish into the "I'll read it later" black hole. A lively Zoom call or an in-person workshop has a better shot at hitting the target.

Step #4: Support with Consistency

Now that you have 7 VIPs and are committed to training, the next question is: How do you ensure people use these systems? The answer is a supportive yet accountable culture that says, "We're not going to be sticklers about everything, but we are going to be unwavering about these seven things."

Accountability sometimes sounds harsh, but think of it as a *healthy partnership rather than policing*. In successful nonprofits, staff and volunteers want clarity on how to deliver their best. Having a well-documented standard helps everyone know what is expected.

Coaching Tip:

Support involves two key levers: assistance and challenge. If people feel they do not have a human resource to assist them, they will opt out. Designate an individual who is trained and can help staff and volunteers in person if possible. Conversely, if someone assumes they can fly under the radar, they will not engage with the system. Conduct personal check-ins with everyone expected to use the system to kindly challenge any lack of participation and deviations. This is not a shaming tactic. However, everyone needs to be challenged to step up. Otherwise, your 7 Very Important Processes become Very Ignored Processes.

Conclusion

Ultimately, the beauty of systems is that they allow your staff and volunteers to focus on what drew them to the nonprofit in the first place: making an impact! Building out your 7VIPs (and sticking to them) might feel like added labor at first, but the payoff is worth it.

Passion without structure can burn bright but often fizzles quickly. Structure without passion might be efficient, but it struggles to connect with hearts. However, when these two tributaries merge, you tap into a powerful river that propels your nonprofit forward.

By taking the time to craft your 7VIPs and following them with a high level of commitment, you build a foundation that can weather staff turnover, funding changes, or unexpected crises. Supporting your staff and volunteers isn't about policing. It's about collectively carrying the torch of the mission in an organized, sustainable way. The other components of the Impact Operating System—Vision, Strategy, Development, Culture, Metrics, People, Rhythms—will flourish when you lay the foundation of consistent, reliable systems.

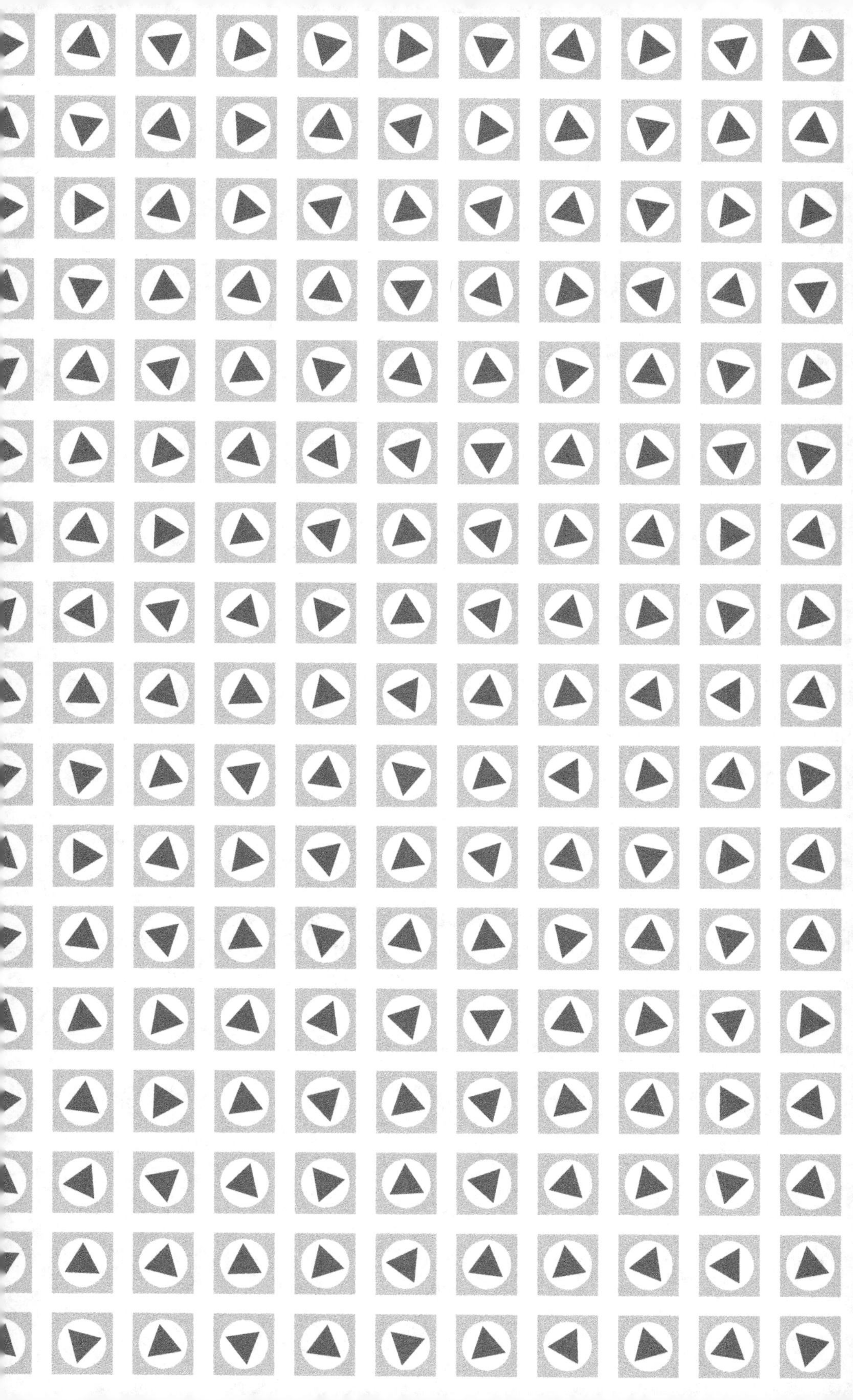

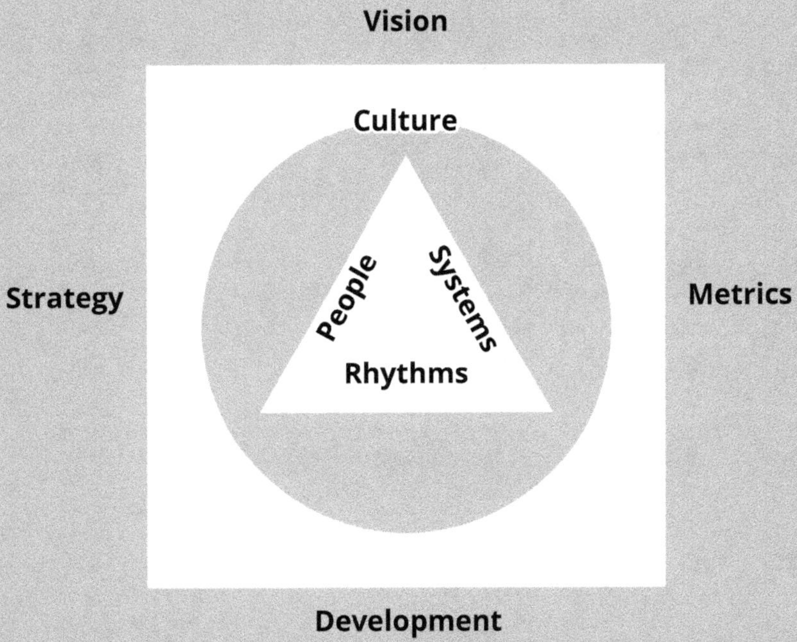

Vision

Culture

Strategy

People

Systems

Metrics

Rhythms

Development

Organizations that set goals with scheduled accountability have a 95% success rate.

10

RHYTHMS

One of the nonprofits we worked with allowed us to observe their weekly staff meeting in real time. Within 20 minutes, the team had veered from addressing the urgent volunteer shortage to selecting paint colors for the foyer (which required unanimous consent) to brainstorming a new marketing slogan. The whiplash was real. It was lively, but a very unproductive use of that meeting.

The average worker spends about 37% of their work time in meetings or coordinating them. No wonder "death by meeting" has entered our work lexicon. So, is the problem that we have regular, rhythmic meetings, or is it the lack of focus and helpful agendas?

As this nonprofit began integrating the principles of the Impact Operating System, we helped them shift their meeting agendas to focus on their priorities. The result? Meetings were cut in half, and yet every critical topic was covered. *The problem wasn't the rhythm; it was the focus.* Oh, and by the way, the paint color banter didn't vanish—it just moved to a designated "sidebar," where it belonged.

More than most organizations, nonprofits need lightweight structures that support clear rhythms and consistent accountability. Every dollar matters, every volunteer hour is precious, and every missed step can ripple out to the vulnerable populations you serve. Good intentions will only get you so far; without consistent follow-through, your mission remains stuck in the realm of aspiration.

In this chapter, we will explore how to weave consistent, life-giving rhythms into your nonprofit's DNA without suffocating your team's passion. Instead, it will free them to focus on where it's needed most. You will see how these rhythms integrate the vital components of the Impact Operating System—Vision, Development, Strategy, Metrics, Culture, People, and Systems—so your team stays on mission without being driven into the ground.

We want to partner with you to turn mission-driven intentions into consistent, sustainable outcomes.

Repeatable Rhythms Lead to Sustainable Impact

Let's begin with a reality that should jolt any nonprofit leader wide awake:

> *When an organization creates goals with a plan and schedules when they will be held accountable, they have a 95% success rate.*

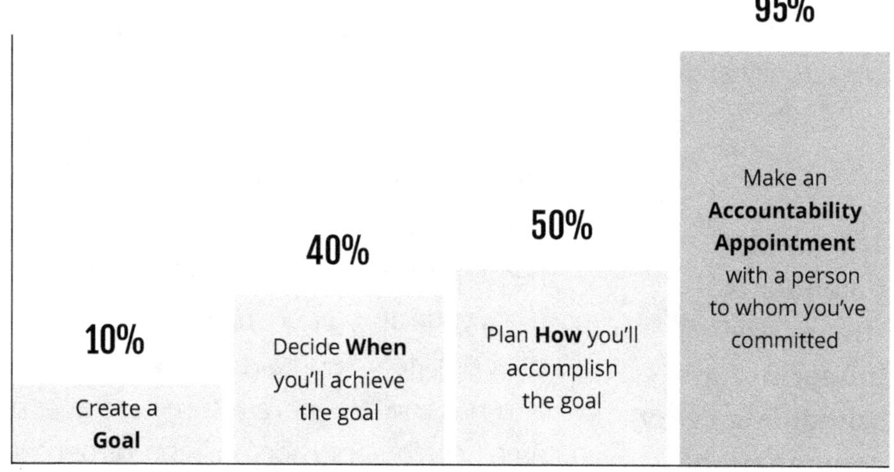

***The American Society of Training and Development**

If you're out to transform your community, why not give yourself the best odds at success?

One stumbling block is the perception that structured routines dampen creativity.

Nonprofits are fueled by passion and empathy, so bringing "function to form" can feel corporate and cold. Well-structured rhythms won't turn your team into robots; they will ensure your life-changing work doesn't get lost in the daily shuffle. Focus will sharpen. Chaos will fade. The mission will take center stage.

The Impact Calendar

The Impact Calendar is the master blueprint for scheduling every component of your customized Impact Operating System for the year. It's your operating system's power strip. It plugs in all the crucial elements—Vision, Development, Strategy, Metrics, Culture, People, and Systems—so they don't remain idle or disconnected.

When you see everything mapped out, you stop wondering, "When will we actually address these ideas?"

The Impact Calendar is the master blueprint for scheduling every component of your customized Impact Operating System.

Imagine waking up on Monday with crystal clarity on when issues will be addressed, when metrics will be reviewed, and which donors need nurturing that week. And yet, within that...you and your team still find plenty of room for spontaneous work, creativity, and passion. No more last-minute guesses or email chain confusion. Instead of perpetually playing catch-up, you step into a more proactive stance. Issues like staff morale, program evaluations, and new fundraising campaigns all have designated moments on the calendar. This is not a pipe dream. It's a real possibility.

As a point of clarification, this is not the same as your organizational calendar that includes volunteer orientations, programming deadlines, etc. While it may be helpful to have them located together so that you are not dealing with the confusion of keeping up with two different calendars, they are not synonymous. The Impact Calendar centers your mission-critical rhythms so that impact, not busyness, drives the week. It's a tool for aligning your calendar with your cause, not just your commitments.

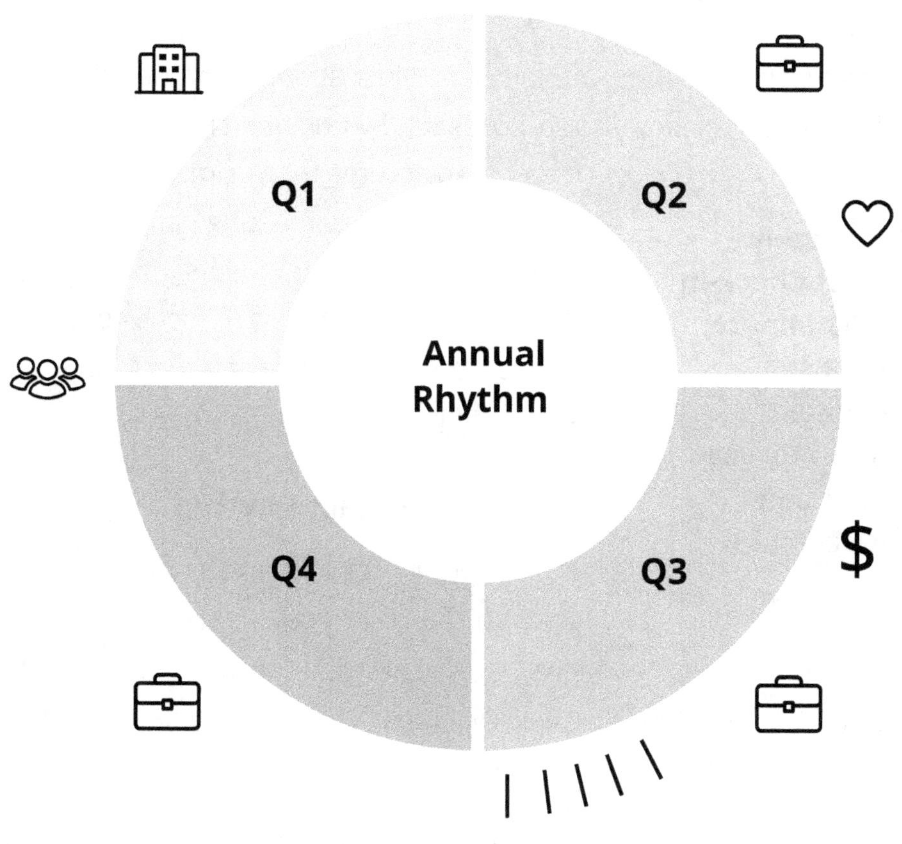

| Weekly Impact Check-in
90 Minutes

Annual Refresh
2 Days

Annual Board Retreat
2 Days

90 Day Goal Reset
3 Hours

Annual Staff Retreat
2 Days

$ Development Playbook Refresh
3 Hours

Four Rhythms of Your Impact Calendar

Let's zoom in on four core rhythms:

1. **Weekly Rhythms**
2. **Monthly Rhythms**
3. **Quarterly Rhythms**
4. **Annual Rhythms**

These types of rhythms are familiar to just about everyone. While that can be advantageous, it also poses its own unique challenge because it is easy to assume this is simply "business as usual" under a new meeting name. However, The Impact Calendar adapts how you use these familiar rhythms by focusing on the mission-critical alignment that promotes sustained impact.

The Weekly Impact Check-In is a 90-minute, no-nonsense alignment session focused on mission-critical tasks.

1. Weekly Impact Rhythm

A nonprofit can make or break its goals in the day-to-day hustle. While annual retreats or monthly reviews are essential, proper accountability usually happens in tight weekly loops. *The Weekly Impact Check-In* is the place where that happens.

This is a 90-minute, no-nonsense alignment session focused on mission-critical tasks. It's a trigger that *jolts* the team into action and is the most important, non-negotiable meeting of the Impact Operating System. We cannot overstate its value. If you consistently use this meeting as designed, you will make the progress needed.

Before diving into the meeting agenda, we need to take a quick look back at the Impact Roadmap and make a couple of additions, as it will be your guide.

Impact Roadmap Refresh

In Chapter 3 (Strategy), we introduced the Impact Roadmap, but we noted it was incomplete and we would come back to it.

At this point, you should refresh yourself with this tool in that chapter. We mentioned that it is a straightforward, adaptable way to fuse big-picture thinking with daily execution. Rather than focusing on endless pages of analysis, it pinpoints your key strategic elements and integrates them into a living document you and your team can use weekly, monthly, and quarterly.

This will be the guide you will use in your Weekly Impact Check-In meetings. So, you will need to have completed this tool. As mentioned, we highly recommend that you co-create this with your team vs. the leader "coming down from the mountain" with the Vision completed as a gift to everyone. Several reasons support this recommendation, not the least of which is the principle: "What people create, they own." This will set your team up for making progress toward the mission.

Impact Roadmap Additions

With that in mind, there are two additions we want to add to the Impact Roadmap that you need during your Weekly Impact Check-Ins. After briefly introducing them to you, we will provide you with a Weekly Check-In Meeting Agenda so you can see and understand the meeting flow.

1. **Issues List**

   These are the challenges that arise out of each of the 90 Day Goals and other things you've identified over the course of the week. When the owner of each goal reports out, they also identify where they are stuck and what they need. You may raise other urgent issues too, even if they are not tied to a 90-day goal, as long as they are relevant and not off-topic. However, merely surfacing the issue is not the goal. We regularly see teams stop short of taking the next important step: taking time in the discussion to Identify, Discuss, and Solve for possible solutions. After surfacing the potential solution, team members are tasked with taking action over the next week and reporting back at the next Weekly Impact Check-In Meeting. If solved, that issue is taken off the board.

2. **Three Weekly Personal Must Wins**

   Every team member identifies three must-wins for their upcoming week that are directly tied to the mission and will move it forward. This is not their personal "to-do list" of daily tasks; rather, it is of greater importance. This gets everyone thinking about and prioritizing their time toward the things that are most "Urgent and Important".

   In Chapter 3: Strategy, we mentioned that the key to lasting, sustainable impact is not to stall at the 90-Day Goals level, but get to ground level by focusing on weekly goals and making it personal for each team member. It's moving from 100,000 feet in the air (your Moonshot) all the way to 5 feet off the ground (your granular, weekly work).

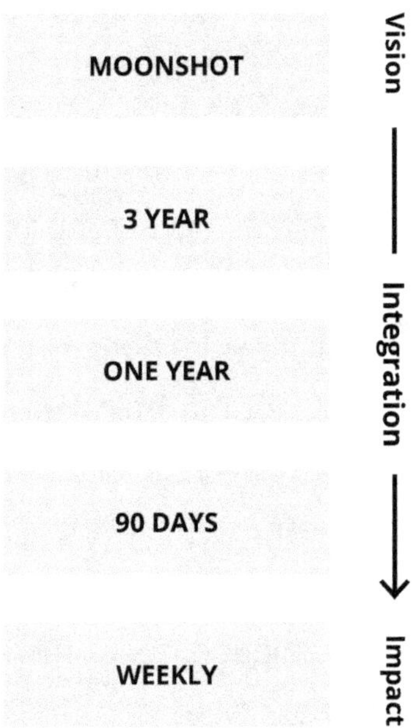

Remember, 93% of nonprofit employees don't understand how the organization's strategy intersects with their everyday work. This is one of the primary factors that diminishes the sense of meaning for staff and, thus, decreases vision, motivation, effort, and productivity. The Weekly Impact Check-In Meeting is designed to combat this problem. In *The 12 Week Year*, authors Brian Moran and Michael Lennington would put it, "Shorter cycles spark urgency. A sprint mindset shatters annual complacency." By setting weekly sprints, your staff will take more decisive steps.

That means everyone—from executive leaders to custodial staff—is identifying their weekly must-wins and connecting their work back to the mission. When done, momentum builds as it creates positive social pressure because no one wants to be the only team member who doesn't follow through.

Now, let's put this all together and look at the Weekly Impact Check-In Agenda.

Weekly Impact Check-In Agenda

1. **Values Story (5 min)**

   In Chapter 6: Culture, we introduced you to the Internal Work Values. This is one place where they begin to take flight. Kick things off with an example of a team member living out your values. This sets an upbeat tone and reinforces the "why" of the organization. When you begin to add this to your rhythm, you will have to prime the pump for stories. Eventually, it becomes something everyone is looking for during the week, and they come excited to share how a team member is embodying your values.

2. **Impact Story (5 min)**

   Not only did we introduce Values in Chapter 6: Culture, but we also introduced you to the power of Narratives. The Weekly Impact Check-In is a designated place to rhythmically share a small but meaningful success. This could be about a client you helped or a volunteer who made a difference. Most of the time, these are not going to be exceptional types of stories, although they could be, of course. These are stories that celebrate small wins and steady service. Remember, what you celebrate will tend to be reinforced and repeated.

3. **90-Day Goals Report Out (15 min)**

   In Chapter 3: Strategy, we introduced you to the 90-Day Goals. They are the activation steps of your 5 Year Moonshot and directly correspond to your 3 Year Milestones. We also noted how each of them needs a champion who, while not solely responsible for completing this goal, ensures it is accomplished. It's at this point in the weekly meeting that the champion/owner of each 90-Day Goal reports on their progress in quick 3-minute snapshots for each update and adds any issues to the Issues List.

4. **Weekly Must Wins Check-In (15 min)**

   Every team member reports out on their 3 Weekly Personal Must Wins by answering the following questions:

   - Did you complete last week's must-wins? Briefly describe.
   - Present your new must-wins for the upcoming week.
   - What needs to go on the Issues List?

5. **Impact Dashboard Check-In (15 min)**

   In Chapter 5: Metrics, we introduced the Impact Dashboard. This is the setting where you examine the core metrics that show how well you're tracking. This is a focused set of metrics (typically 9 to 15) that capture what matters most to your organization. These are not just data points; they tell the story of your progress toward meaningful outcomes. A team member will need to be designated with ensuring these metrics are updated for each meeting.

6. **Identify/Discuss/Solve Issues (30 min)**

   As the meeting progresses, you'll identify issues you need to solve. Don't solve them immediately; add them to the Issues list, and move on. Spend 30 minutes in the meeting to work through the most significant obstacles on the table and tackle them one by one to find solutions, or you may need to find another space to solve other issues that arise.

7. **Debrief the Meeting (5 min)**

   This is a quick reflection on the meeting itself. It is not a rehash of what has already been discussed, but a way to ensure your meetings accomplish their purpose by asking, "What went well in this weekly check-in and what can we improve to make it as effective as possible?"

Weekly Impact Check-In Best Practices

1. If you're using the ImpactHub app, have everyone open it so they can follow along, share their Must Wins, add to the group Issues List, and view the Dashboard. If you're not using the app, print out a double-sided Weekly Check-in Agenda Worksheet such as the one below. This will keep everyone on the same page. (You'll find this document in the Starter Kit linked by the QR code in the Introduction of this book.)

2. If you are not using our ImpactHub app or another digital platform, print out or use a digital version of your Impact Dashboard so everyone can see the updated numbers in black and white.

3. Consistency is king. So, here are five rules to follow:

    - Rule #1: Keep the meeting on the same day weekly
    - Rule #2: Keep the meeting at the same time weekly
    - Rule #3: Follow the same meeting format and use a printed or digital worksheet
    - Rule #4: Start on time
    - Rule #5: End on time

Resources for Your Weekly Check-In

You need two 8.5″ x 11″ pages to lead your Weekly ImpactCheck-In.

1. A completed Impact Roadmap
2. A Weekly Impact Check-In Agenda

5 Year

Impact Strategy

IF (Strategy), THEN (Moonshot).

3 Year

Milestone 1	Milestone 2	Milestone 3	Milestone 4

1 Year

One Year Must Win

90 Days

Goal 1	Goal 2	Goal 3	Goal 4

Issues List	3 Weekly Personal Must Wins
Identify / Discuss / Solve	

Vision → Integration → Impact

Weekly Impact Check-In Agenda

Values Story Story of breakthrough in how we work together	**5 Min.**
Impact Story Story of breakthrough through our mission	**5 Min.**
90-Day Goals Report Out *3 minutes per goal	**15 Min.**
Weekly Must Win Check-in *Review last week's wins - Did you win? • Here's where I won • Here's where I lost • Here's where I'm stuck (add to issues list)	**15 Min.**
Impact Dashboard Check-in	**15 Min.**
Review To Do List	**5 Min.**
Solve Issues List	**30 Min.**
Debrief the Meeting	**30 Min.**

Additional Notes

2. Monthly Impact Rhythms

One of the most overlooked but profoundly impactful, repeatable rhythms in any organization is the regular one-on-ones between a leader and their direct reports. Part of the beauty of the Impact Operating System is its customization: if your team is spread thin and relatively autonomous, quarterly may be adequate. But if you are navigating more dynamic situations – like a fast-changing program environment or staff who need closer coaching – a monthly check-in can be a lifesaver.

These one-on-ones create a structured environment where the individual employee feels seen, heard, and supported. Much like the Weekly Impact Check-In, they foster accountability and clarity of direction. Unlike the team meeting, however, these sessions go deeper into personal performance, professional development, and the everyday roadblocks someone might be too shy (or insecure) to address publicly. By setting aside thirty to sixty minutes a month, you create a space for growth and reflection that can significantly boost morale and drive consistent results.

Monthly Check-In Agenda

1. **Win/Learn Check-In (5 minutes):**

   Kick off by asking, "What's a win you're proud of since we last spoke?" Follow up with "What's something you learned about yourself, the mission, or the work?" This sets a positive tone and reinforces continuous improvement.

2. **Review Current Goals and Must-Wins (10–15 minutes):**

   This is where you check progress on quarterly goals and weekly must-wins. Ask about obstacles, offer guidance, and make sure the direct report sees how their weekly tasks align with the broader Vision.

3. **Discuss Any Obstacles or Issues (10–15 minutes):**

   Create a safe space for your team members to share frustration, confusion, or concerns. Some issues may need to go on the master Issues List if they affect the broader team, but others can be resolved with a bit of coaching or resource allocation.

4. **Right Fit Reflection (5–10 minutes):**

   Every few one-on-ones, take time to explore fit. Ask: "Is there any part of your role, rhythm, or team dynamic that feels especially energizing or frustrating lately?" Use this to surface insights about alignment, engagement, and growth.

5. **Professional Development & Feedback (5–10 minutes):**

   Whether it's building a new skill or addressing performance gaps, use this time to coach. Simple, specific feedback shows you're invested in that person's growth.

6. **Next Steps (5 minutes):**

   Wrap up with a concise plan. What are the key takeaways or actions before the next one-on-one?

While it may seem like just another meeting on the calendar, a well-run one-on-one can dramatically strengthen the relationship between the team member and direct report. When employees know there's a consistent platform for voicing concerns and celebrating wins, they feel more invested in their work and their professional development. That sense of engagement and partnership drives better execution, helping your nonprofit move forward with energy and focus. Note: Some leaders determine that this rhythm is better suited to a quarterly cadence.

3. Quarterly Impact Rhythms

Every quarter, schedule a deeper strategic review. This meeting gives you time to evaluate performance, address deeper issues, and ensure you're still heading in the right direction.

You'll want a reasonable amount of time to do this, so the space has room to breathe and you can have a deeper discussion without feeling like you have to plow through it.

Quarterly sessions keep you consistent, preventing the whiplash of big surges followed by neglect. In this quarterly time together, you're going to evaluate your last 90 days, set new 90-day goals, and build on the learning from the previous quarter into the latest quarter.

Quarterly Strategic Session Agenda (3 hours):

1. **Celebrate**: Value & Impact Stories – Start with good vibes.
2. **Review Metrics**: What story do these numbers tell us about the last quarter, and what does it mean about the next?
3. **Review Previous 90-Day Goals**: Did you accomplish them? If not, why?
4. **Establish New 90-Day Goals**: Where should energy go next?
5. **Review & Solve Issues**: Allocate enough time to unearth root causes, not just symptoms.
6. **Review Task List with Timelines:** Ensure the goals you set are reasonably achievable and agreed upon with accountability in place.
7. **Closing Thoughts:** Give your team a motivational send-off into the next quarter.

Encourage and expect honest dialogue here. Celebrate the goals that were accomplished and boldly name the ones missed. Determine why you missed goals (i.e., unrealistic targets, lacking resources, etc.). Learn from this and move forward with clarity and confidence.

4. Annual Impact Rhythms

Annual planning typically evokes images of a big retreat where staff gather, hopefully away from day-to-day distractions. Going on a yearly staff retreat is not exactly a revolutionary idea. While it's often beneficial, what's crucial is how you use that time. Spend some of it reflecting on the past year. However, don't get stuck in review. Look at your Impact Roadmap and set the following year's must-win that aligns with your 3-year milestones and 5-year Moonshot.

Combine this annual session with a thorough overview of your Impact Operating System. This isn't just a calendar exercise. It's your chance to recalibrate the entire Impact Operating System for the year ahead. When you intentionally revisit each of the eight components, you create alignment across your organization. Vision gets translated into updated milestones. Strategy shifts from abstract to actionable. Development plans are matched with revenue needs. Metrics are refined to track what matters. Culture gets a health check. People are assessed for role and structure fit. Systems are tightened or simplified. And rhythms, like your Impact Calendar, are reloaded for the coming year. This isn't maintenance; it's mission-tuning.

Without this annual rhythm, most nonprofits default to drifting by reacting to fires instead of steering toward a future. But when you align your one-year goals to the core architecture of your operating system, you activate organizational coherence. Everyone, from board members to new staff, can see how their role fits into the big picture. The retreat becomes more than a feel-good getaway; it becomes a strategic engine that drives real momentum. The ImpactOS is not static; *it's dynamic*. And the annual planning retreat is the moment you upgrade it for maximum mission alignment.

Coaching Tip:

Break the 24 hours across two days. For instance, meet from 1–5 p.m. on Day 1, then reconvene from 9 a.m. to 12 p.m. on Day 2. Something magical happens while people sleep: things settle overnight and you wake up with more clarity. The evening in between is priceless for informal connections, deeper conversations, or downright fun activities that bond your team. This fosters an environment where brainstorming and strategic thinking are lively and collaborative, rather than forced. You can use informal meal times (like dinner on Day 1) to share stories of breakthroughs related to your values and the mission. Let these meals and sharing linger in a way where it doesn't feel like it's driving an agenda forward.

If We Haven't Convinced You Yet

If all of this hasn't been quite enough to get you to commit to some basic repeatable rhythms for execution, maybe this will push you over the top:

> *In our work with nonprofits, we have found that those that maintain a consistent weekly execution rhythm and re-evaluate their goals quarterly have, on average, seen a 40% uptick in donor retention.*

Why?

Because donors will feel and see the effects that you are organized and making tangible strides. No one likes throwing money into chaos. This goes well beyond retaining donors. It's about showing that each dollar given is being stewarded responsibly through transparent, measurable steps. In the eyes of supporters, consistent execution rhythms make your nonprofit trustworthy, stable, and mission-focused, increasing the likelihood they will stick around for the long haul.

You know what else? It makes your work that much more meaningful and fun.

Conclusion

Jim Collins and Morten T. Hansen relayed a story called "The 20 Mile March" in their book *Great by Choice*. In 1911, two expeditions raced to the South Pole—one led by Roald Amundsen, the other by Robert Scott. Amundsen's team marched a set distance (roughly 15–20 miles) every day, regardless of weather conditions, never pushing in good weather or slacking off in bad.

In contrast, Scott's team swung between exhausting sprints on favorable days and near-total rests on poor ones. Amundsen's consistent pace proved decisive, enabling him to outlast harsh conditions and achieve his goal first.

From this example, Collins and Hansen coined "20 Mile March" as a metaphor for disciplined, steady progress toward a set performance target.

Instead of sprinting in good times and stalling in bad, organizations should commit to a set performance target they strive to hit consistently. This approach builds resilience, preventing both burnout and complacency. Over time, these incremental steps compound to outperform other methods that rely on dramatic but unsustainable bursts of effort. Consistency wins over dramatic spurts.

By customizing and integrating an *Impact Calendar* that includes weekly check-ins, quarterly reviews, and an annual planning session, you breathe consistency and energy into your Moonshot. The other components of the Impact Operating System—Vision, Strategy, Development, Culture, Metrics, People, and Rhythms—gain new life, ensuring consistent follow-through.

So, embrace the rhythms, trust the process, and watch as clarity and alignment elevate your nonprofit towards remarkable, sustained impact. In a world brimming with unmet needs, your capacity to execute consistently is the difference between another hopeful idea and a transformed community.

11

INTEGRATION

After making it this far, you may be asking, "I can definitely see the benefit this could bring, but who is responsible for carrying the ImpactOS forward in my nonprofit?"

We're glad you asked because the answer to this question is not a minor detail. It may just be the most critical decision you make.

The People Who Make It Work: The Pioneer and the Builder

No matter how helpful the Impact Operating System is, no matter how well it's designed, how comprehensive the tools, or how inspiring the Vision, it won't sustain itself without the right people leading the charge. That's why every nonprofit must identify two core champions to steward this work. We call them The Pioneer and The Builder.

These roles aren't titles on an org chart. They are functions—distinct, complementary roles that keep momentum alive and mission aligned.

The Pioneer = Visionary

The Pioneer is the person who dreams big, sees what's possible before anyone else can, and isn't afraid to knock down walls to get there. They're often the founder, executive director, or senior leader. Their strength is vision, passion, and future-casting. They're the ones who say, "This doesn't exist yet...but it should!" They bring the energy to galvanize people around what's next.

If you mapped the Pioneer using Patrick Lencioni's *Working Genius* framework, you would often find them thriving in Wonder (W), Invention (I), and Galvanizing (G):

- They *wonder* about how the world could be better.
- They *invent* new ways forward.
- They *galvanize* people to join them.

In short: They see it. They create it. They rally others to believe in it.

But big dreams alone won't get you to your Moonshot. You need someone who can translate that Vision into a sustainable, grounded reality.

The Builder = Implementor

The Builder is your implementor. They are detail-oriented, systems-savvy, and relentless about follow-through. This person takes the Pioneer's high-altitude strategy and anchors it into day-to-day execution. They oversee meeting rhythms, accountability loops, metrics analysis, and ongoing momentum. They are not just a task manager. They are the *operational conscience* of the organization, ensuring the machine runs, even on days when passion is low.

In *Working Genius* language, Builders excel in Discernment (D), Enablement (E), and Tenacity (T):

- They *discern* what ideas are workable and when.
- They *enable* others by removing obstacles and setting clear paths.
- They *tenaciously* drive initiatives across the finish line.

In short: They vet it. They mobilize it. They actualize it.

Pioneer Role	Builder Role
Dream it	Ground it
Inspire action	Sustain action
Expand possibilities	Protect momentum
See around corners	Manage what's right in front

This dynamic is inspired by the "Visionary + Integrator" model from *Rocket Fuel*, and fortunately, it translates beautifully to nonprofit life. In fact, we would argue it's even more crucial in the nonprofit space, where impact is the ultimate goal.

For some organizations, this looks like the relationship between an Executive Director and the Director of Operations. For others, it might be the ED and another staff member who is leaning into the function of their role.

But here's the key to ImpactOS success: *The roles and responsibilities only work when they are explicitly agreed upon.*

Too many nonprofits have a Pioneer who thinks they're leading solo, or a Builder who's quietly doing all the grunt work without shared clarity or credit. That's a fast track to burnout and broken trust. It's no coincidence that organizations bring us in to lead a one-day workshop for just these two people! They are, in many ways, the rate-determining factor as to whether an organizational operating system will succeed or crash and burn.

For the ImpactOS to succeed, these two leaders must be in lockstep. That means:

- They both know their roles.
- They have discussed what each of them does well.
- They are aware of where they might clash and how to navigate that terrain.
- And most importantly, they have been released to lead in these roles with clarity and authority.

But these two kinds of leaders can make mistakes, can't they? Of course. They are human.

The Pioneer's biggest mistake is swinging between micromanaging every detail and disappearing entirely. Both extremes leave the Builder frustrated, disoriented, and unable to maintain consistent momentum.

The Builder can also exhibit some undermining tendencies. First, they can become overly rigid, protecting the system at the expense of adapting to evolving opportunities. Second, the Builder might unintentionally under-communicate progress, leaving the Pioneer feeling disconnected and tempted to intervene unnecessarily.

However, when the Pioneer and Builder operate in complete alignment, the whole organization feels it. The engine that is the ImpactOS starts to hum and move smoothly and with momentum. Meetings get sharper. Execution gets faster. And momentum builds – because everyone has a Moonshot *and* a Map to get there.

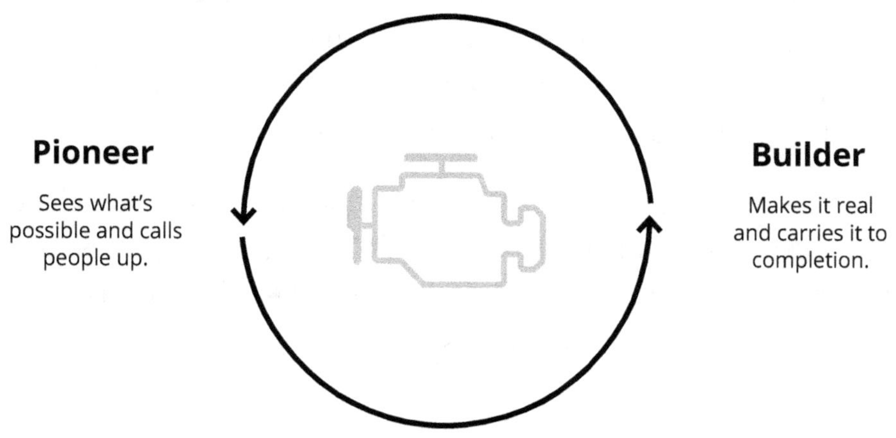

So, as you prepare to integrate the OS into your organization, ask yourself: Who's our Pioneer, and who is our Builder?

Name them. Empower them. Align them.

Because if those two are united, everything else can follow.

The Process That Makes This Work

Hopefully, you are walking away with fresh clarity, renewed energy, and a deep understanding of possibility for what comes next. Maybe your notebook is filled with ideas and action steps like "Talk to Sarah about using the Board Tune-Up Tool at the next meeting" or "Revise onboarding before Q2." Those aren't just scribbles; they're seeds of transformation.

Over the past chapters, you've just immersed yourself in a world of frameworks, tools, case studies, and aha moments. The question is no longer if you can transform your organization, but *how*.

How will you bring these ideas into team meetings, donor conversations, and board retreats?

How will you build a culture where clarity, accountability, and purpose guide every person and every decision?

Picture your staff knowing exactly how their work contributes to the mission. Picture your volunteers feeling seen, valued, and empowered. Picture your board moving past old ruts and toward bold, generative thinking. The Impact OS is designed to help you achieve those realities, no matter the size or stage of your organization.

We desire to help you sustain the momentum long after you close this book and return to the hustle and heart of your organization. So, if you are wondering how to bring the ImpactOS into the day-to-day life of your nonprofit, here is the process we use at the Impact Co.

The ImpactOS Integration Process

This process is specifically designed to keep things lightweight and low maintenance, because the last thing any of us needs is an overengineered integration process that feels more like a burden than a blessing.

Our underlying philosophy is that significant change does not have to be painfully complicated. With the right approach, it can be both meaningful and enjoyable for everyone involved.

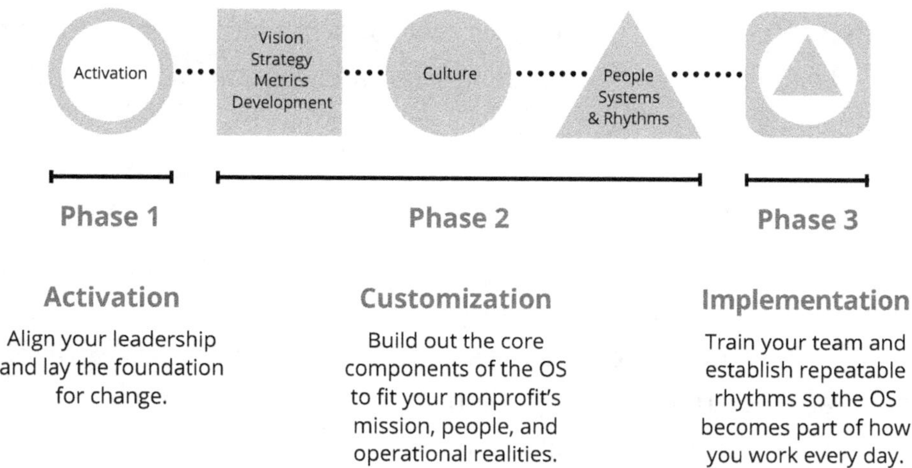

Phase 1: Activation

Wins of This Phase

The primary goal here is to ensure that your organization's core leaders understand why a formal Operating System matters and what the implementation process entails. You want them to appreciate how these tools—like goal-setting rhythms, meeting structures, and accountability frameworks—will ultimately free them to excel in their roles. It's a bit like showing everyone the treasure map before you begin the journey.

Pitfalls

- *The New Fad Syndrome:* If you present the ImpactOS as the latest "shiny object," people may feel cynical or even resistant, as if they're being forced into an experimental process.

- *Leaving Out Key People:* If you don't invite the right stakeholders, especially those who will drive daily operations or cultural norms, you risk implementing a system no one owns or believes in.
- *All Head / No Heart:* Choosing to have an organizational operating system makes all the sense in the world. But most team members of a nonprofit are motivated by heart and passion. Make sure their heart is activated, not just their head.

Why It Matters

Whether you're an established nonprofit with a multi-layered staff or a scrappy startup with a few volunteers, Phase 1 sets the tone. It's your chance to unify everyone around a shared Vision. By the end of Activation, your team should be nodding their heads in agreement, saying, "Yes, we see how this can help us fulfill our mission far more effectively."

Phase 2: Customization

Wins of This Phase

Now you get into the nuts and bolts. During Customization, you and your team adapt the various ImpactOS tools to your organization's unique DNA. You will tweak specific templates, create custom categories that reflect the nuances of your mission, or fill your dashboards in ways that resonate with your people. When done right, Customization ensures the OS feels tailor-made for your nonprofit rather than importing a cookie-cutter approach.

Pitfalls

- *Dominating Voices:* One or two individuals might push their agenda, overshadowing diverse perspectives. Be sure to welcome feedback from across the organization (staff, board, donors, and volunteers) to avoid a top-heavy or lopsided result.

- *Insufficient Familiarity:* If you aren't comfortable using the tools in practical scenarios, like actual meetings or planning, then customization will be superficial.
- *Lack of Iteration:* This is not a "one and done" phase. Expect to experiment, gather feedback, and refine. Without enough feedback loops, you risk finalizing decisions that don't work.

Why It Matters

This phase is like choosing furniture for your living room. Anyone can buy a couch, but the difference between a cozy, personalized space and a sterile showroom often comes down to thoughtful customization. In the same way, the Impact OS should feel like a natural extension of how your nonprofit operates, not an alien set of rules.

Phase 3: Implementation

Wins of This Phase

By this phase, your organization is starting to develop a shared sense of ownership of the OS for planning, reviewing progress, making decisions, and managing. The ultimate milestone: *You can't imagine running your nonprofit without it.* Even better, key team members become confident enough to "apprentice" others, spreading best practices throughout every corner of your organization.

Pitfalls

- *Old Habits Die Hard:* It's easy to slip back into the style of endless, unproductive meetings if you don't consciously anchor your new rhythms. That's why there is a 5-minute debrief at the end of every Weekly Impact Check-In.
- *Untrained Leaders:* If managers who are supposed to champion the OS don't feel trained, confident, equipped, and supported,

they might inadvertently undermine it by reverting to old habits or changing it in ways that differ significantly from the original Vision.

Why It Matters

Integration is about momentum and sustainability. This is when you see your staff self-organizing with minimal confusion, your board trusting the new processes, and your donors and volunteers praising the clarity of communication. In other words, you are harvesting the fruits of all that Activation and Customization labor.

Why a Guide Matters

One of the most common pitfalls for a nonprofit CEO/ED is trying to lead and facilitate this change simultaneously. If you are in this role or the founder, your voice will naturally carry the most weight. Even with the best intentions, it can feel like you are driving an agenda that others have to accept. We've all felt that tension; it comes with the territory. A trusted outside facilitator lets you be a participant who shapes the future with your team, not the person running the meeting. That shift lowers defensiveness, invites genuine input rather than performative agreement, and turns the process into something the team builds and owns together. And because people help create the system, they understand it and feel responsible for keeping it strong.

If that resonates and you would like our help, here are two simple ways we can guide you through Activation, Customization, and Implementation without adding complexity or burden. We have created two distinct pathways that work for nonprofits of all budgets and sizes.

Option #1: The ImpactLite (3-Day Kickstart Cohort)

Best for teams who don't want to do it alone but aren't ready for full support yet.

This is like a boot camp with a seasoned trainer. Bring your three-person team and join other nonprofits for a high-impact, 3-day workshop experience. You will walk away with team-wide alignment and a solid start to customizing your ImpactOS. It will give you a burst of momentum as you start your process.

Why It Works

You get alignment and momentum in days, not months. It helps you down the road quickly and gives you what you need to finish the rest on your own.

Scan the QR code to get more info about the ImpactLite option.

Option #2: The ImpactPro (12-Month Full Integration)

Best for organizations that want a partner every step of the way, delivering results and a system that becomes second nature.

You get a personal Impact Strategist who walks alongside your team for a whole year to tailor the Impact Operating System to your unique context, ensure full implementation, and embed the rhythms, habits, and tools that create lasting impact.

Why It Works

This is our gold standard. With a 95% success rate, ImpactPro embeds habits and tools until they become completely normal for your organization and team.

Scan the QR code to get more info about the ImpactPro option.

ImpactHub App

Your entire customized operating system can live and breathe on this app, just as you have built it. You can run your Weekly Impact Check-Ins from it, see your updated Dashboard, post notes from one-on-ones, annual reviews, meetings, input your Weekly Must Wins...and a whole lot more. The entire app is built specifically for the ImpactOS. Its use is restricted to those who engage in either the *ImpactLite* or the *ImpactPro*.

To get more info, check out: ImpactNonprofit.com/app

If You Get Stuck, Reach Out!

Let's wrap this up by speaking straight from the heart.

You have a dream—something that lit a fire in you long before you picked up this book. Maybe it's ending homelessness in your city, ensuring every child gets an equitable education, rescuing the helpless from sex trafficking, making sure kids in remote villages have access to clean drinking water, or bringing the arts to underserved communities. That dream is precious, and the world desperately needs it to flourish. The ImpactOS is here to help you realize that Vision faster, with fewer distractions and more clarity.

But dreams don't always follow a neat, straight line. If you find yourself stalled at any point—if you are unsure how to get staff on board, if a board member resists the new approach, or if you simply can't seem to figure out a meeting rhythm that works—please remember: you're not alone. The entire reason we exist is to help people like you deliver world-shifting impact.

Keep pressing in. Don't miss your moment. Change is hard; friction is normal. You're not just adding a meeting; you're shifting how your nonprofit thinks and operates. That takes a different kind of sustained energy. If you want a steady hand as you take on this challenge, we are just an email, text, Zoom, or phone call away, ready to troubleshoot, encourage, and celebrate with you.

The Real Risk Isn't Change. It's the Status Quo.

The real risk is doing nothing. When Vision stays on paper, drift sets in. Meetings fill the calendar but not the scoreboard. Good people burn out. Donors grow uncertain because they cannot see progress. Opportunities pass by while everyone waits for "someday." Momentum doesn't just stall; it leaks. And over time, teams learn the wrong lesson: impact is optional here.

You can have a compelling Vision, a winning strategy, and all the funding you need, but without a simple system that supports that Vision, you will not consistently do great things.

It doesn't have to be that way.

ImpactOS is a nonprofit-specific playbook that helps you realize the Vision you carry with a system that has heart, stays human, and amplifies passion instead of draining it.

Remember, the most successful nonprofits share eight components. We built a simple operating system around them so the right things become the easy things: a focused plan everyone can see, a weekly rhythm your team can keep, clear owners who deliver, and a set of measures that actually guide decisions. The result will be less scramble, more progress; less personality drag, more shared ownership; less talk, more traction.

You don't need to overhaul everything. You need light structure that fits your reality and brings clarity, alignment, and a cadence that people can keep. That's what the eight components give you when they run together. And when they do, the work feels different. Staff leave meetings knowing what's next. Volunteers feel seen and useful. Boards move from rut to responsibility. Donors see outcomes they can trust. The community you serve feels the difference.

This is the work of leadership: to make it normal for the right things to happen. To build a system that carries the weight of your calling without crushing your people. To choose a pace your team can sustain so your mission can endure.

Your Next Step

You started this journey because something in the world needs to change. The tools are in your hands. The process is clear. The support is available. Name your Pioneer and Builder. Start the weekly check-in. Tie your metrics to decisions. Invite your team to co-own the system you are building together.

You do not need more hype. You need a system that matches the size of your heart for this cause.

Let's build that system: one decision, one conversation, one rhythm at a time.

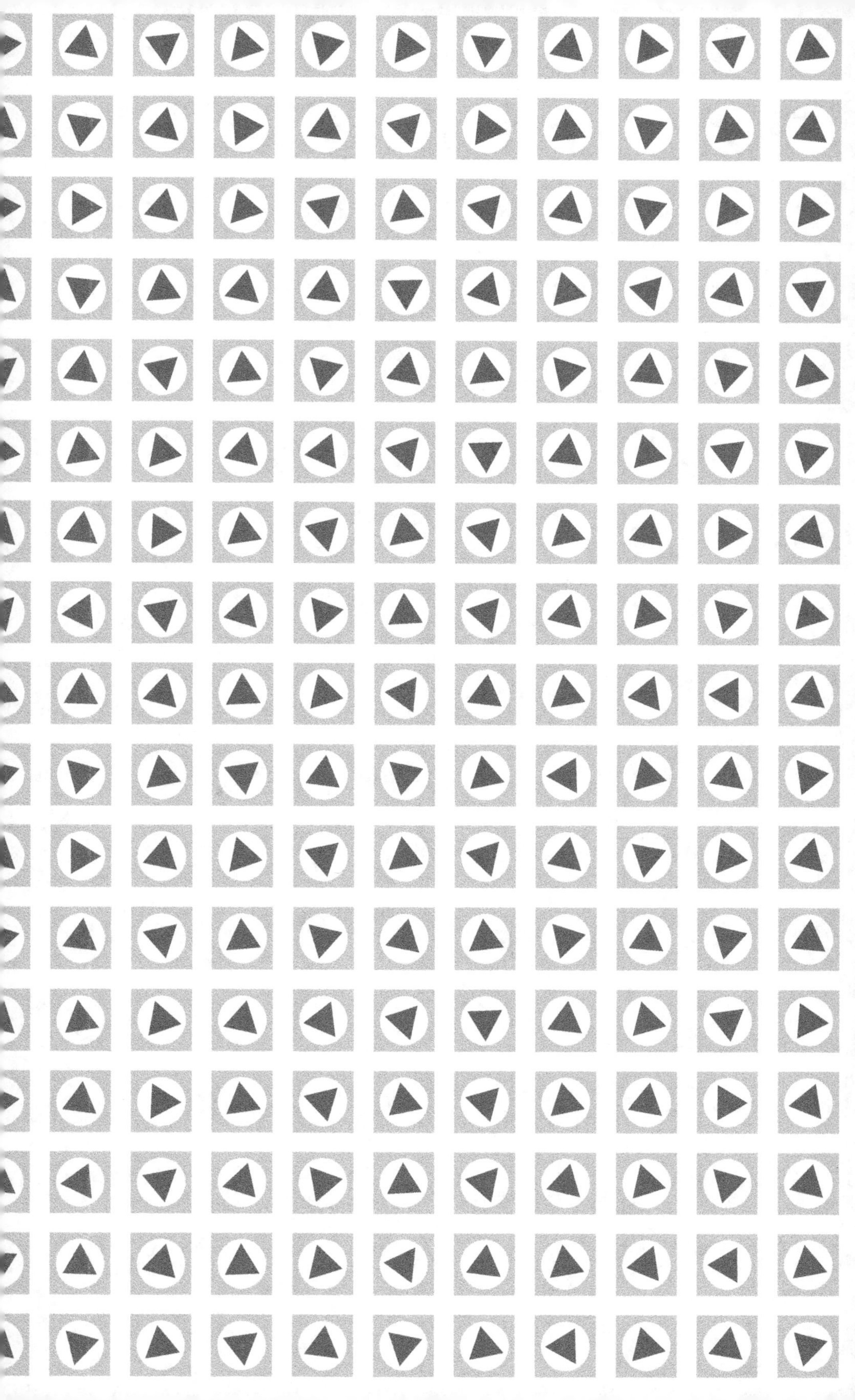

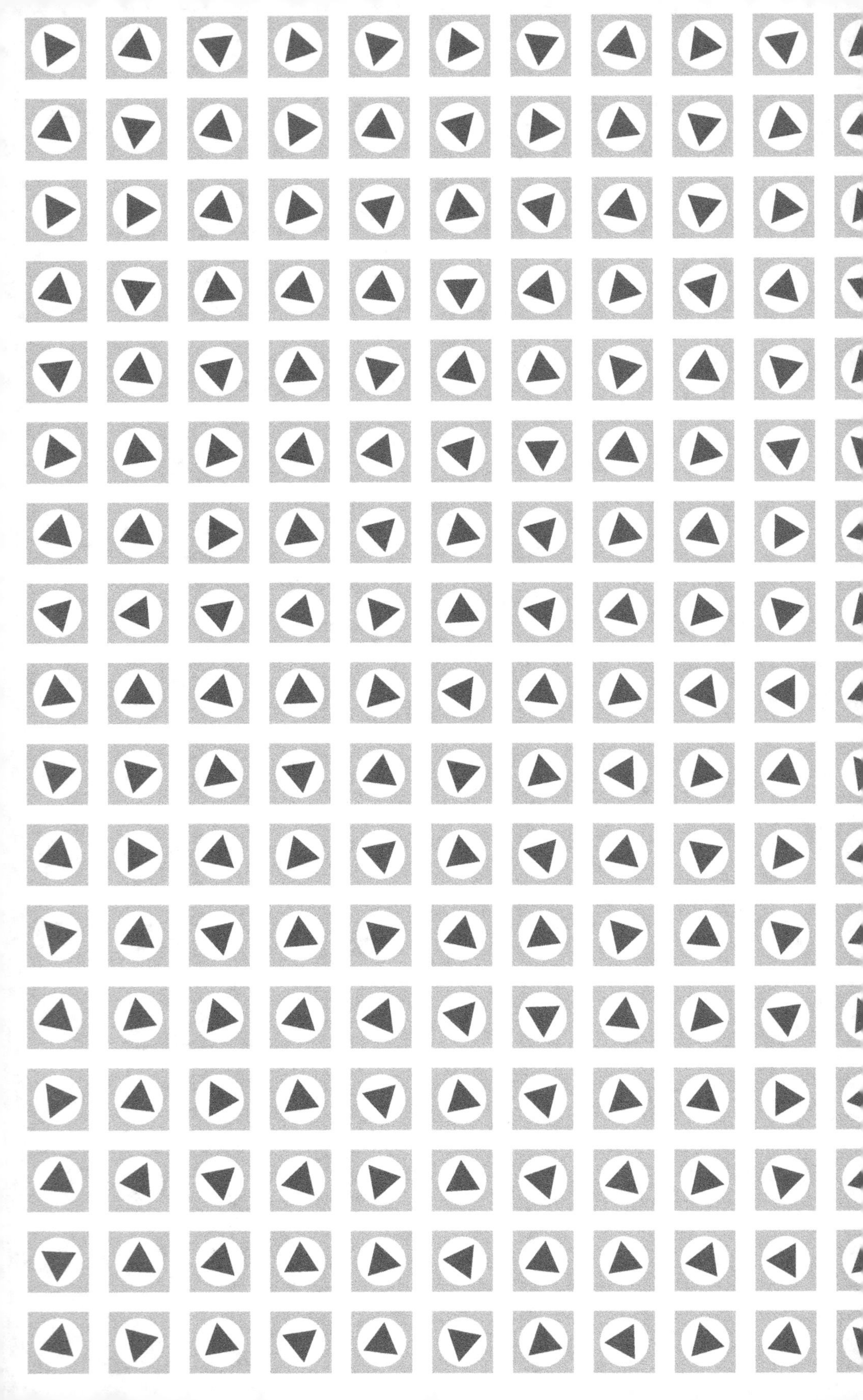

GLOSSARY OF TERMS

Successful Nonprofit:

A successful nonprofit is an organization whose mission is genuinely transformative for the people it serves, whose culture is so healthy that team members want to stay and contribute, and whose operations are sustainable enough to keep the organization strong with finances that are growing and predictable.

Organizational Operating System:

A holistic set of rhythms, roles, decisions, and tools that determine how your organization actually functions day to day.

Vision:

A preferred picture of the future.

Moonshot:

A measurable, time-bound slice of your Vision.

Strategy:

How you get from Point A (where you are now) to Point B (your Moonshot).

Impact Strategy:

A single, testable statement that captures how you believe you'll win. "If we focus on X, then Y will happen." It's your strategy boiled down to conviction.

Impact Roadmap

A flexible strategic action plan that connects your Moonshot to real execution through 3-Year Milestones, a One-Year Must Win, 90-Day Goals, and Weekly Action Steps.

Change Theory:

A theory of change is your best, evidence-informed explanation of how and why your work leads to real change. It connects the dots between your activities, your outcomes, and the long-term transformation you're aiming for.

Development:

Aligns your fundraising approach with your vision and values, creating a sustainable plan that invites donors into the story of impact.

Development Formula:

Sustainable Development = Right-sized Bandwidth + Updated Playbook + Rhythmic Triggers

Metrics:

The 9-15 things you count that give you a 360-degree picture of your organization at any given time (organizationally & missionally).

Aspirational Values:

The qualities your organization hopes to embody in the future but doesn't consistently demonstrate today.

External Values:

The values you intentionally promote to the outside world to shape your public identity and signal what matters to your mission.

Internal Work Values:

The shared commitments that define how your team chooses to work together daily.

Culture:

"Whatever is normal for a group of people."

People:

The key stakeholders in a nonprofit who occupy different seats on "the bus" and need to work in alignment, clarity, and trust – Staff, Board, Donors, Volunteers, Partners.

Compensation Formula:

Compensation = Money + Meaning

Systems:

The very important processes you use over and over again that give you a disproportionate amount of operational lift.

Very Important Process (VIP):

The operational heartbeat of your nonprofit: the 20% of your daily operational tasks that yield 80% of your results. It's the engine that keeps your operations running smoothly. Each VIP typically involves multiple steps, stakeholders, and a predictable order of actions. It's "very important" because, without it, your mission stalls.

Rhythms:

The repeatable patterns you use for setting goals, holding each other accountable, and solving problems together.

Pioneer:

The visionary leader who sees the future before it exists. Catalytic, intuitive, and built to push boundaries.

Builder:

The operational leader who makes vision executable. Steady, systems-oriented, and committed to finishing what gets started.

80/20 Execution Principle:

If something is 80% clear, aligned, and resourced, it's time to start. We don't wait for perfection to make progress. We move when we're mostly aligned, and let the remaining 20% emerge through real-world testing, feedback, and iteration—not endless planning.

Pareto Principle:

Roughly 80% of your results come from 20% of your effort. In a nonprofit context, a small number of actions, relationships, or programs are likely driving the majority of your impact, donations, or engagement. The rest? Noise, distraction, or diminishing returns.

Lead Measure:

A lead measure is a controllable, predictive action or input that influences future performance and helps drive progress toward a goal.

Lag Measure:

A lag measure is an outcome-based result that reflects past performance and shows whether a goal has been achieved.

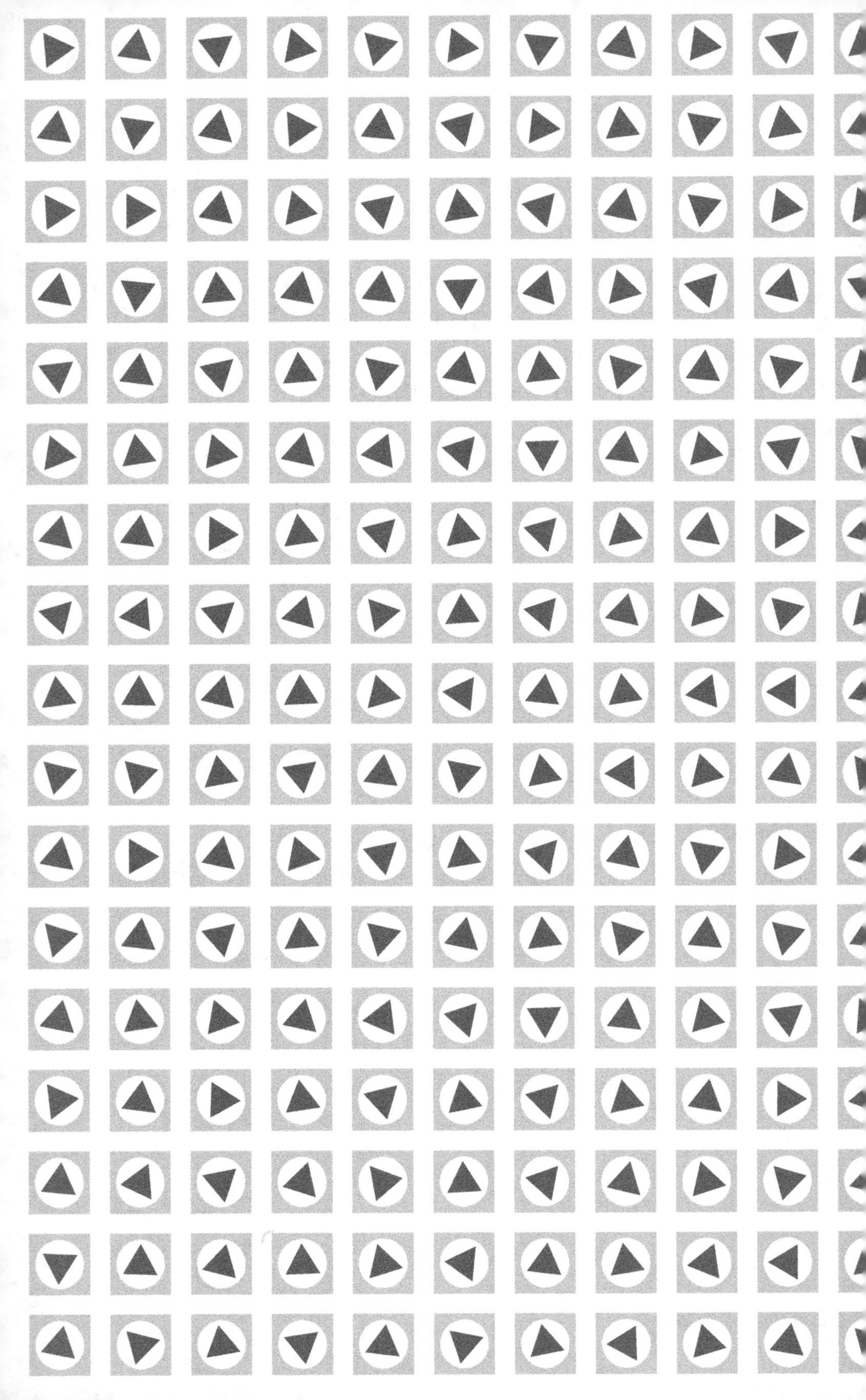

TOOLS SUMMARY

Overview of ImpactOS

Component	What's Required	Master Tool	Problem this is Trying to Solve
Vision	A clear, 5-year, attainable slice of the big vision	Moonshot Tool	Your vision sounds good but you're getting luke-warm results.
Strategy	A flexible action plan linked to a winning strategy.	Impact Roadmap	Your team is really busy but you're not getting momentum.
Development	A modern revenue playbook built for your DNA.	FUEL Matrix	Every year it's harder to raise the same amount of money.
Metrics	A scorecard with lead and lag impact measures.	Impact Dashboard	You're not sure you're measuring the right things in the right way.
Culture	Shared agreement on "how we work together."	Culture Making Tool	Unintentional culture undermines great teams.
People	The right people in the right seats of the bus.	Right Fit Tool Org Chart Analyzer DARCI Board Tune Up Tool	Role confusion and bottlenecks across staff, board, and volunteers.
Systems	Simple, repeatable core processes documented and followed.	7 VIP Tool	Dropped balls, last-minute scrambles, and something is always on fire.
Rhythms	Repeatable cadences that trigger impact outcomes.	Impact Calendar	Inconsistent execution, quality, and accountability.

Vision: Moonshot Tool (Chapter 2)

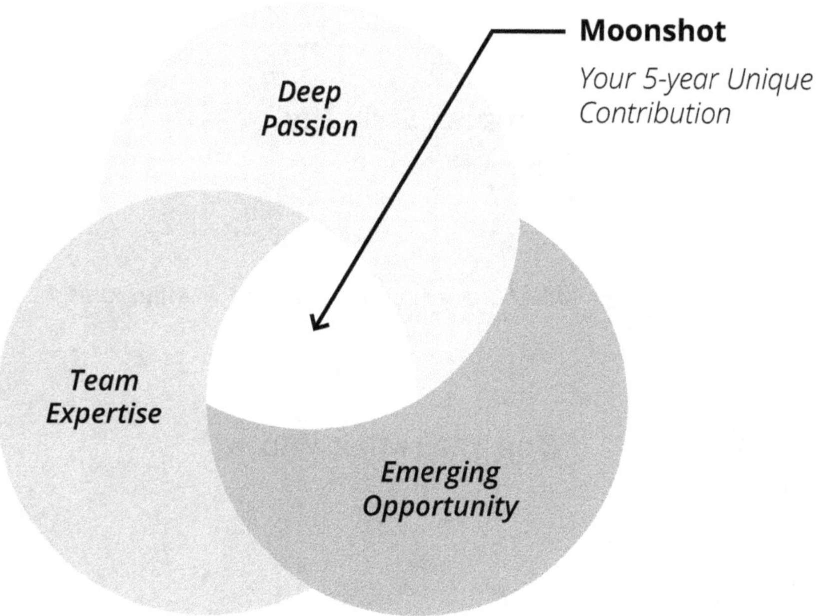

Strategy: Impact Roadmap (Chapter 3)

Development: FUEL Matrix (Chapter 4)

	Operations	Technology	Data & Insights	Relation-ships	Campaigns	Education	Storytelling	Thank You Culture	Alternative Revenue
101 Tactics									
201 Tactics									
301 Tactics									
401 Tactics									

Metrics: Impact Dashboard (Chapter 5)

Category

Lead Measures

METRIC 1

METRIC 2

Lag Measures

METRIC 3

Culture Making Tool (Chapter 6)

P	L	A	N

People: The Right Fit Tool (Chapter 7)

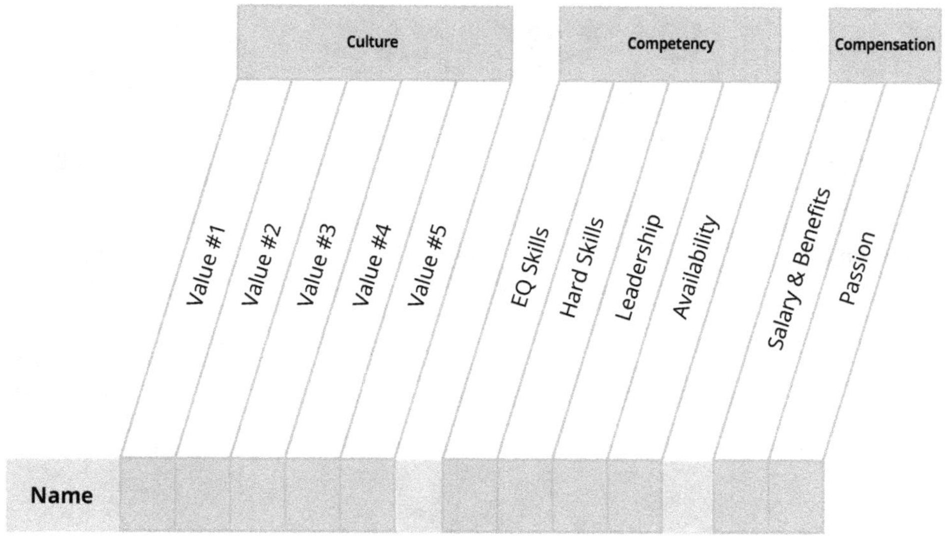

People: The Board Tune Up Tool (Chapter 7)

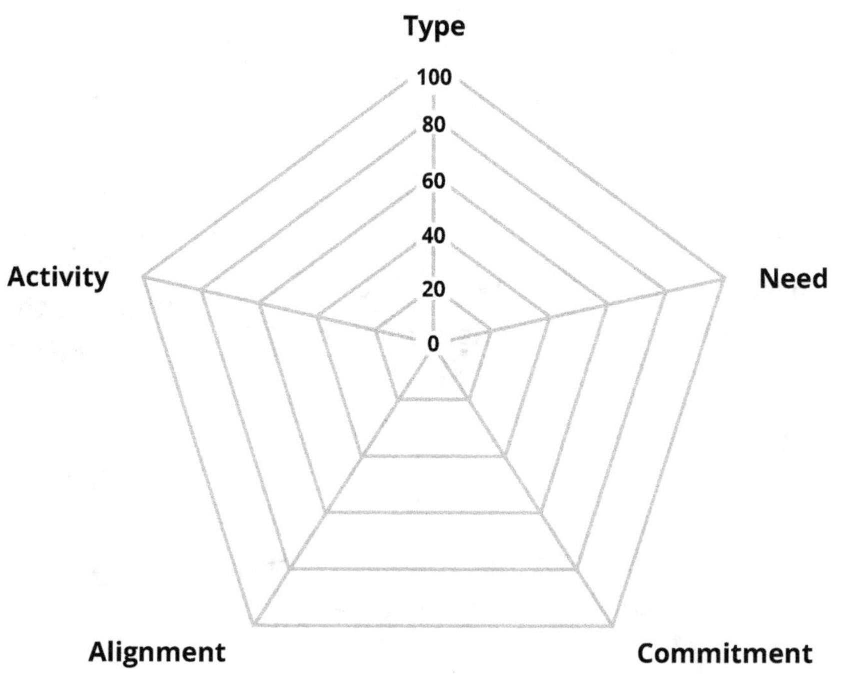

People: The DARCI Framework (Chapter 8)

Organizational Function	D Decision Maker	A Accountable	R Responsible	C Consulted	I Informed
Fundraising					
Function 2					
Function 3					
Etc.					

People: The Org. Chart Analyzer (Chapter 8)

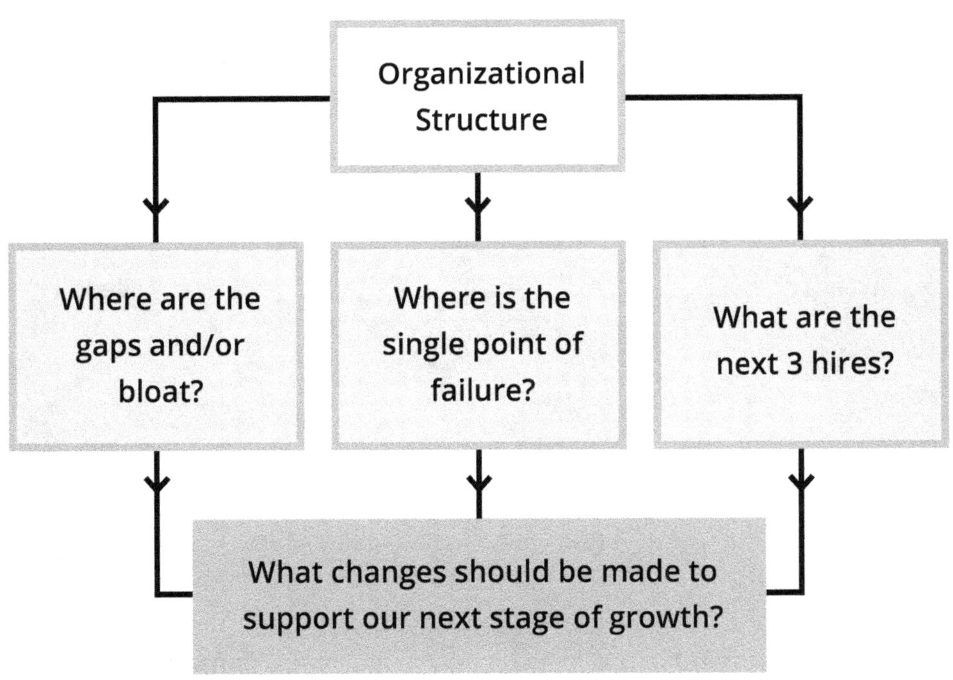

Systems: The 7VIP Tool (Chapter 9)

Rhythms: The Impact Calendar (Chapter 10)

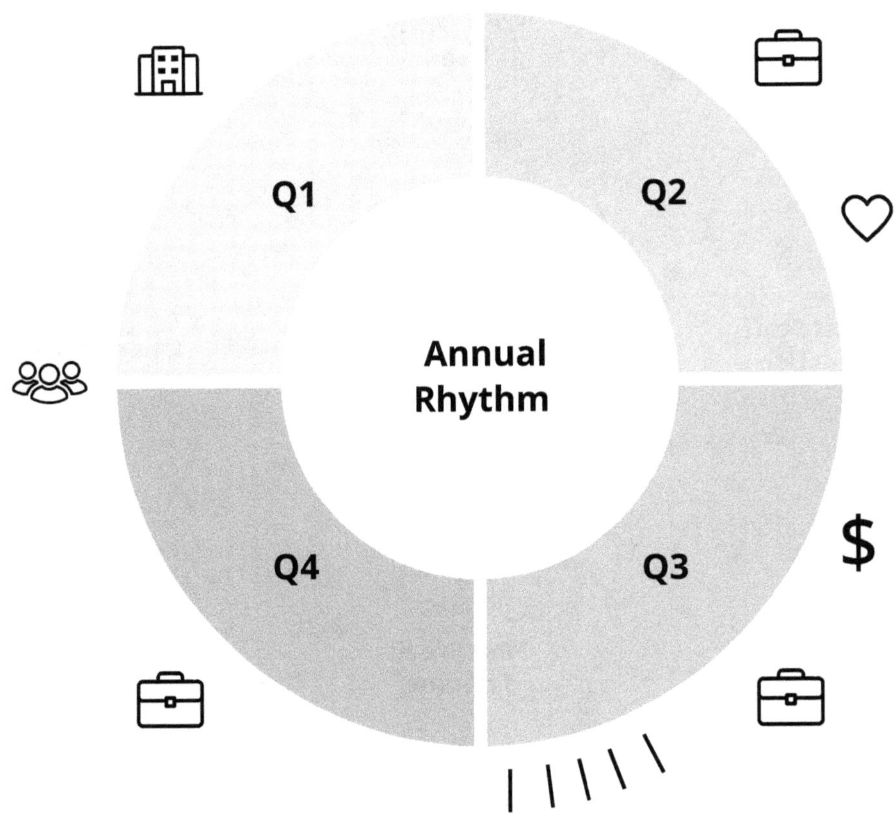

	Weekly Impact Check-in 90 Minutes		90 Day Goal Reset 3 Hours

- **Weekly Impact Check-in** 90 Minutes
- **Annual Refresh** 2 Days
- **Annual Board Retreat** 2 Days
- **90 Day Goal Reset** 3 Hours
- **Annual Staff Retreat** 2 Days
- $ **Development Playbook Refresh** 3 Hours

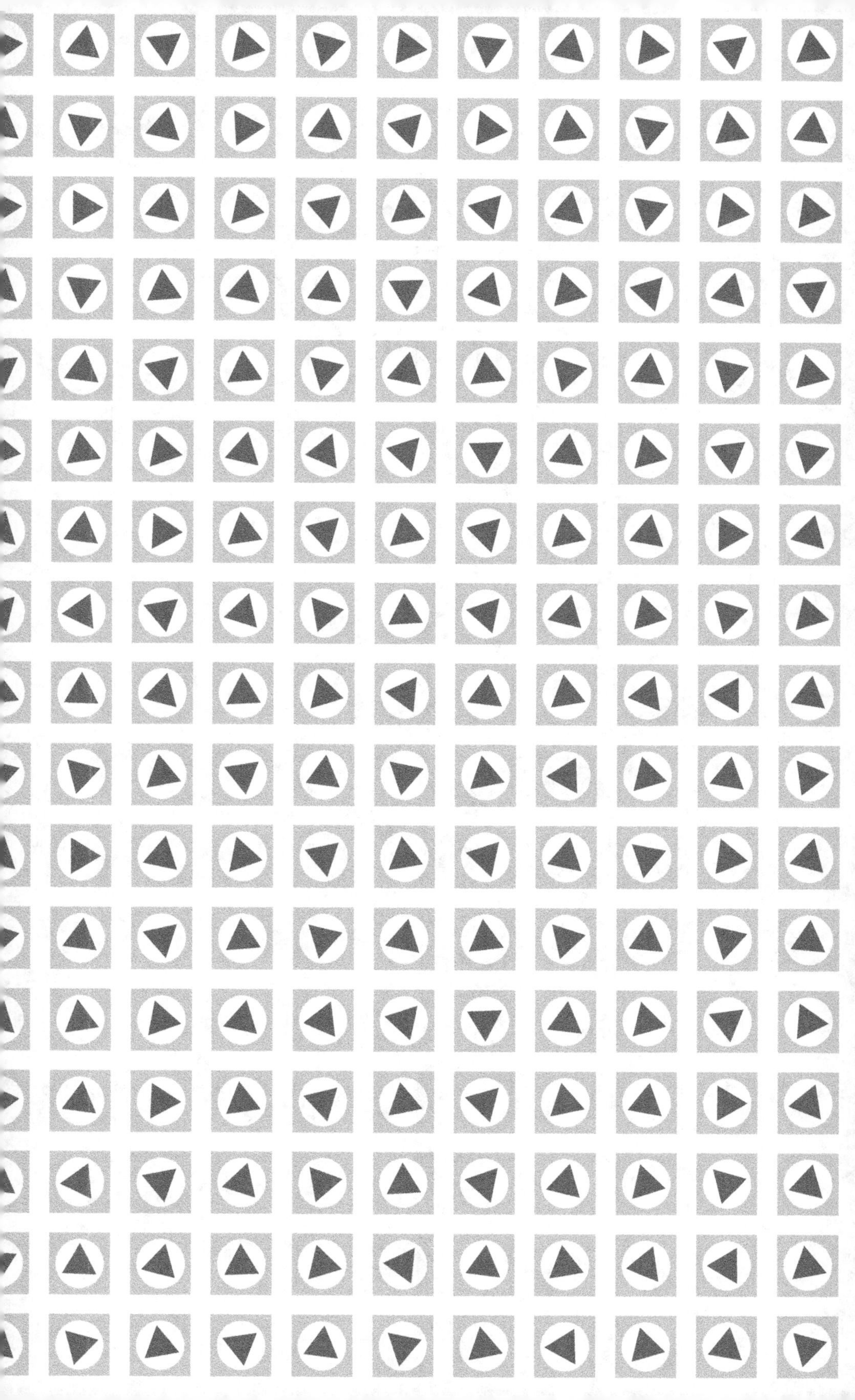

END NOTES

End Notes Introduction

This book draws on real-world experiences from years of working alongside nonprofit leaders, teams, and organizations. To honor the privacy and confidentiality of those involved, the names, roles, and identifying details have been changed throughout.

Chapter 1 – Introducing the ImpactOS

71% of nonprofits are currently failing at their stated mission – National Council of Nonprofits. *Nonprofit Impact Matters: How America's Charitable Nonprofits Strengthen Communities and Improve Lives.* National Council of Nonprofits, 2019.

This is an adaptation of the original quote: "You do not rise to the level of your goals. You fall to the level of your systems." Clear, James. *Atomic Habits: An Easy & Proven Way to Build Good Habits & Break Bad Ones.* Avery, 2018.

Wickman, Gino. Traction: *Get a Grip on Your Business.* BenBella Books, 2011.

Chapter 2 – Vision

20% of nonprofits feel they have a Vision that's propelling them in a positive direction. National Development Institute. *Reimagining Philanthropy*. National Development Institute, Whitepaper.

Lencioni, Patrick. *The Advantage: Why Organizational Health Trumps Everything Else in Business*. Jossey-Bass, 2012.

Kennedy, John F. "Special Message to the Congress on Urgent National Needs." Address, U.S. Capitol, May 25, 1961. John F. Kennedy Presidential Library and Museum.

Shallenberger, Steve. *Becoming Your Best: The 12 Principles of Highly Successful Leaders*. Berrett-Koehler Publishers, 2014.

Collins, Jim. *Good to Great and the Social Sectors: A Monograph to Accompany Good to Great*. Jim Collins, 2005.

Nanus, Burt. *Visionary Leadership: Creating a Compelling Sense of Direction for Your Organization*. Jossey-Bass, 1992.

Hyatt, Michael. *The Vision Driven Leader: 10 Questions to Focus Your Efforts, Energize Your Team, and Scale Your Business.* Baker Books, 2020.

Other books on Vision that have shaped our thinking we recommend:

Simon Sinek, "Start with Why: How Great Leaders Inspire Everyone to Take Action" (Portfolio, 2009).

Steve Shallenberger, "Becoming Your Best: The 12 Principles of Highly Successful Leaders" (McGraw-Hill, 2014).

Jim Collins and Jerry I. Porras, "Built to Last: Successful Habits of Visionary Companies" (HarperBusiness, 1994).

Burt Nanus, "Visionary Leadership: Creating a Compelling Sense of Direction for Your Organization" (Jossey-Bass, 1992).

Andy Stanley, "Visioneering: Your Guide for Discovering and Maintaining Personal Vision" (Multnomah, 2005).

Chapter 3 – Strategy

86% of nonprofits with a clear fundraising strategy experience increased results. Ryan, Eric. 2020 *State of Nonprofit Strategy Report*. Mission Met, 2020.

Rumelt, Richard. *Good Strategy/Bad Strategy: The Difference and Why It Matters*. Crown Business, 2011.

Pollard, Mark. *Strategy Is Your Words: A Strategist's Fight for Meaning.* Sweathead, 2023.

Harnish, Verne. *Mastering the Rockefeller Habits: What You Must Do to Increase the Value of Your Growing Firm*. Gazelles, Inc., 2002.

The Patterson Center for Resiliency, LLC. *The Patterson Center for Resiliency*. Colorado Springs, CO.

Kaplan, Robert S., and David P. Norton. *The Balanced Scorecard: Translating Strategy into Action*. Harvard Business School Press, 1996.

Auxano. *Auxano: Church Consulting / Visionary Planning.* Chelsea, AL: Auxano, Inc.

Wickman, Gino. *Traction: Get a Grip on Your Business.* BenBella Books, 2011.

(OKRs) – Grove, Andrew S. *High Output Management*. Random House, 1983.

(Cascading) – Drucker, Peter F. *The Practice of Management.* Harper & Row, 1954.

Other books on Strategy that have shaped our thinking we recommend:

W. Chan Kim and Renée Mauborgne, "Blue Ocean Strategy: How to Create Uncontested Market Space and Make the Competition Irrelevant," Expanded ed. (Harvard Business Review Press, 2015).

A. G. Lafley and Roger L. Martin, "Playing to Win: How Strategy Really Works" (Harvard Business Review Press, 2013).

Clayton M. Christensen, "The Innovator's Dilemma: When New Technologies Cause Great Firms to Fail" (Harvard Business School Press, 1997).

Robert S. Kaplan and David P. Norton, "The Balanced Scorecard: Translating Strategy into Action" (Harvard Business School Press, 1996).

Geoffrey A. Moore, "Crossing the Chasm: Marketing and Selling Disruptive Products to Mainstream Customers," 3rd ed. (HarperBusiness, 2014).

Chapter 4 – Development

30% of nonprofits will shut down in the next decade due to financial instability. National Center for Charitable Statistics. *The Nonprofit Sector in Brief.* Urban Institute, 2021.

Jerold Panas, Born to Raise: What Makes a Great Fundraiser Great, 30th Anniversary ed. (Toronto: Civil Sector Press, 2023).

Other books on Development that have shaped our thinking we recommend:

Kim Klein, "Fundraising for Social Change," 7th ed. (Wiley, 2016).

Penelope Burk, "Donor-Centered Fundraising," 2nd ed. (Cygnus Applied Research, 2018).

Laura Fredricks, "The Ask: How to Ask for Support for Your Nonprofit Cause, Creative Project, or Business Venture," Updated & Expanded ed. (Wiley, 2010).

Ilona Bray, "Effective Fundraising for Nonprofits: Real-World Strategies That Work," 8th ed. (Nolo, 2025).

Adrian Sargeant and Elaine Jay, "Fundraising Management: Analysis, Planning and Practice," 3rd ed. (Routledge, 2014).

Chapter 5 – Metrics

29% of nonprofits accurately measure their impact. Candid. *Measuring Impact: Nonprofit Perspectives on Effectiveness.* Candid.org, 2020.

Peter F. Drucker, "The Practice of Management" (Harper & Brothers, 1954).

Beth Kanter and Katie Delahaye Paine, "Measuring the Networked Nonprofit: Using Data to Change the World" (Jossey-Bass/Wiley, 2012).

Mario Morino, "Leap of Reason: Managing to Outcomes in an Era of Scarcity" (Venture Philanthropy Partners, 2011).

Other books on Metrics that have shaped our thinking we recommend:

Mary Kay Gugerty and Dean Karlan, "The Goldilocks Challenge: Right-Fit Evidence for the Social Sector" (Oxford University Press, 2018).

Marc J. Epstein and Kristi Yuthas, "Measuring and Improving Social Impacts: A Guide for Nonprofits, Companies, and Impact Investors" (Berrett-Koehler, 2014).

Chari Smith, "Nonprofit Program Evaluation Made Simple: Get Your Data. Show Your Impact. Improve Your Programs" (Business Expert Press, 2021).

Alison Green and Jerry Hauser, "Managing to Change the World: The Nonprofit Manager's Guide to Getting Results," 2nd ed. (Jossey-Bass, 2012).

David E. K. Hunter, "Working Hard—and Working Well: A Practical Guide to Performance Management" (Results1st, 2013).

Chapter 6 – Culture

Nonprofits with intentional, healthy cultures see a 43% increase in productivity. Eagle Hill Consulting. *The Case for Culture: Driving Productivity in Nonprofits*. Eagle Hill Consulting, 2023.

There are over 2.5 million seniors who are homebound in the U.S. Wenting Peng et al., "Digital Technology Use in US Community-Dwelling Seniors With and Without Homebound Status," *Journal of the American Medical Directors Association*, Nov. 2024.

Simon Sinek, "Leaders Eat Last: Why Some Teams Pull Together and Others Don't" (Portfolio, 2014).

Daniel Coyle, "The Culture Code: The Secrets of Highly Successful Groups" (Bantam, 2018).

Other books on Culture that have shaped our thinking we recommend:

Liz Wiseman, "Multipliers: How the Best Leaders Make Everyone Smarter," Rev. & updated ed. (Harper Business, 2017).

Andy Crouch, "Culture Making: Recovering Our Creative Calling" (InterVarsity Press, 2008).

Clotaire Rapaille, "The Culture Code: An Ingenious Way to Understand Why People Around the World Live and Buy as They Do" (Broadway Business, 2006).

Daniel H. Pink, "Drive: The Surprising Truth About What Motivates Us" (Riverhead Books, 2009).

Stanley McChrystal, Tantum Collins, David Silverman, and Chris Fussell, "Team of Teams: New Rules of Engagement for a Complex World" (Portfolio, 2015).

Dave Logan, John King, and Halee Fischer-Wright, "Tribal Leadership: Leveraging Natural Groups to Build a Thriving Organization" (Harper Business, 2008).

Charles Duhigg, "The Power of Habit: Why We Do What We Do in Life and Business" (Random House, 2012).

Wendy Griswold, "Cultures and Societies in a Changing World," 4th ed. (SAGE Publications, 2013).

Chapter 7 – People Part 1

93% of nonprofit staff don't understand how their work connects to the organization's strategy. Funding for Good. "Surprising Statistics About Strategic Planning." *Funding for Good*, Feb. 24, 2023.

Peter Bregman, "Big Arrow Strategy Guide" (Bregman Partners, 2016).

Wickman, Gino. *Traction: Get a Grip on Your Business.* BenBella Books, 2011.

John Carver, "Boards That Make a Difference: A New Design for Leadership in Nonprofit and Public Organizations," 3rd ed. (Jossey-Bass, 2006).

82% of volunteers and staff report feeling undervalued. – Johnson Center for Philanthropy. "The Nonprofit Workforce Is in Crisis." Johnson Center for Philanthropy, 2023.

Other books on People Part 1 that have shaped our thinking we recommend:

Richard P. Chait, William P. Ryan, and Barbara E. Taylor, "Governance as Leadership: Reframing the Work of Nonprofit Boards" (Jossey-Bass, 2005).

Peter F. Drucker, "Managing the Nonprofit Organization: Principles and Practices" (HarperCollins, 1990).

BoardSource, "The Nonprofit Board's Role in Human Resource Management" (BoardSource, 2010).

Victor Futter and Daniel L. Kurtz, "Nonprofit Governance and Management," 4th ed. (American Bar Association, 2011).

David O. Renz, ed., "The Jossey-Bass Handbook of Nonprofit Leadership and Management," 4th ed. (Jossey-Bass, 2016).

Chapter 8 – People Part 2

59% of nonprofit employees cite their organizational structure as a primary reason for leaving their positions. Nonprofit Leadership Alliance. Nonprofit Workforce Trends Report. Nonprofit Leadership Alliance, 2023.

Brené Brown, "Dare to Lead: Brave Work. Tough Conversations. Whole Hearts." (Random House, 2018).

Christine W. Letts, William P. Ryan, and Allen Grossman, "High Performance Nonprofit Organizations: Managing Upstream for Greater Impact" (John Wiley & Sons, 1998).

Other books on People Part 2 that have shaped our thinking we recommend:

Mary Tschirhart and Wolfgang Bielefeld, "Managing Nonprofit Organizations: Principles and Practice" (Wiley-Blackwell, 2012).

Leslie R. Crutchfield and Heather McLeod Grant, "Forces for Good: The Six Practices of High-Impact Nonprofits," Revised & Expanded ed. (Jossey-Bass, 2012).

Darian Rodriguez Heyman, ed., "Nonprofit Management 101: A Complete and Practical Guide for Leaders and Professionals," 2nd ed. (Wiley, 2019).

Steve McCurley and Rick Lynch, "Volunteer Management: Mobilizing All the Resources of the Community," 3rd ed. (InterPub Group, 2006).

David E. K. Hunter, "Working Hard—and Working Well: A Practical Guide to Performance Management" (Results1st, 2013).

Chapter 9 - Systems

26% of the average nonprofit staffer's day is wasted on inefficient tasks. FormAssembly. *The State of Nonprofit Data Collection 2021.* FormAssembly, 2021.

Paarlberg, Laurie E., and Roseanne M. Mirabella. "Voluntary Turnover in Nonprofit Human Service Organizations: The Impact of High Performance Work Practices." International Journal of Public Administration 38, no. 5 (2015): 372–385. https://www.researchgate.net/publication/279225456_Voluntary_Turnover_in_Nonprofit_Human_Service_Organizations_The_ Impact_of_High_Performance_Work_Practices

National Council of Nonprofits. 2023 Nonprofit Workforce Survey Results. October 2023. https://www.councilofnonprofits.org/files/media/documents/2023/2023-nonprofit-workforce-survey-results.pdf

Verne Harnish, "Scaling Up: How a Few Companies Make It... and Why the Rest Don't (Rockefeller Habits 2.0), Revised 2025." (Gazelles Inc., 2025).

Wickman, Gino. Traction: Get a Grip on Your Business. BenBella Books, 2011.

Atul Gawande, "The Checklist Manifesto: How to Get Things Right" (Metropolitan Books, 2009).

Other books on Systems that have shaped our thinking we recommend:

Sam Carpenter, "Work the System: The Simple Mechanics of Making More and Working Less," 3rd ed. (Greenleaf Book Group Press, 2018).

Atul Gawande, "The Checklist Manifesto: How to Get Things Right" (Metropolitan Books, 2009).

James P. Womack and Daniel T. Jones, "Lean Thinking: Banish Waste and Create Wealth in Your Corporation," Updated & expanded ed. (Free Press, 2003).

Mike Michalowicz, "Clockwork: Design Your Business to Run Itself," Revised & expanded ed. (Portfolio, 2022).

John Warrillow, "Built to Sell: Creating a Business That Can Thrive Without You" (Portfolio, 2011).

Chapter 10 – Rhythms

Organizations that set goals with scheduled accountability have a 95% success rate. American Society for Training and Development. *The Power of Writing Down Goals and Accountability*. ASTD, 2010.

The average worker spends about 37% of their work time in meetings or coordinating them. - Hailey Mensik, "The true cost of meetings, by the numbers," WorkLife, April 25, 2024.

Hailey Mensik, "The True Cost of Meetings, by the Numbers," *WorkLife*, April 25, 2024, https://www.worklife.news/culture/the-true-cost-ofmeetings-by-the-numbers/

93% of nonprofit employees don't understand how the organization's strategy intersects with their everyday work. – Funding for Good. "Surprising Statistics About Strategic Planning." *Funding for Good*, Feb. 24, 2023.

Brian P. Moran and Michael Lennington, "The 12 Week Year: Get More Done in 12 Weeks than Others Do in 12 Months" (Wiley, 2013).

Jim Collins and Morten T. Hansen, "Great by Choice: Uncertainty, Chaos, and Luck—Why Some Thrive Despite Them All" (HarperBusiness, 2011).

Other books on Rhythms that have shaped our thinking we recommend:

Larry Bossidy and Ram Charan, "Execution: The Discipline of Getting Things Done" (Crown Business, 2002).

Chris McChesney, Sean Covey, and Jim Huling, "The Four Disciplines of Execution" (Free Press, 2012).

Andrew S. Grove, "High Output Management," rev. ed. (Vintage, 1995).

John Doerr, "Measure What Matters: How Google, Bono, and the Gates Foundation Rock the World with OKRs" (Portfolio, 2018).

Jeff Sutherland, with J. J. Sutherland, "Scrum: The Art of Doing Twice the Work in Half the Time" (Crown Business, 2014).

Chapter 11 – Integration

Gino Wickman and Mark C. Winters, "Rocket Fuel: The One Essential Combination That Will Get You More of What You Want from Your Business" (BenBella Books, 2015).

Patrick M. Lencioni, "The 6 Types of Working Genius: A Better Way to Understand Your Gifts, Your Frustrations, and Your Team" (Matt Holt Books, 2022).

impactco. helps nonprofits get unstuck and grow their impact. We partner with mission-driven leaders to build the clarity and structure that makes momentum sustainable. So you can turn a "nice vision" into vision with teeth, build a team people want to be part of and do not want to leave, and grow funding alongside sustainable, working operations. Our core framework, the Impact Operating System, brings these pieces together into a simple, repeatable playbook you can run with your team.
ImpactNonprofit.com

www.ingramcontent.com/pod-product-compliance
Lightning Source LLC
LaVergne TN
LVHW010649110826
845149LV00014B/3004
9798993527505